the **big things**
in life are the
little things

GENE LOGSDON
STEVE ZENDER

the big things
in life are the
little things

SLOWLANE PUBLISHERS
1198 E. FINDLAY STREET
P.O. BOX 37
CAREY, OHIO 43316-0037

Slowlane Publishers
1198 E. Findlay Street
P.O. Box 37
Carey, OH 43316-0037

a collection

This volume is a collection of works by Gene Logsdon and Steve Zender from 1974 to the present. Most of the selections are from weekly newspaper columns, Logsdon's "Country Rover" and Zender's "Small-Town Boy," written for The Progressor-Times in Carey, Ohio.

cover art

Years ago when The Progressor-Times office was in downtown Carey, I often walked to work from my home on E. Findlay Street. I went to work early, usually, depending upon the season, about daybreak. From the quiet, dark distance I could see the warm light streaming out of My Place Restaurant and I could see the row of vehicles – sometimes entirely made up of pickup trucks – along the curb.

I could not actually see the sunrise from where I was, but often, as I looked back over my shoulder, I would notice the orange of the new day brightening the old buildings along the way. I rarely stopped to eat, and I hardly ever saw My Place customers coming or going, but as I passed by, I could see them sitting at the tables inside, eating their bacon and eggs, sipping their coffee. They were reading newspapers. Joking. Arguing. Gossiping. They were hashing over the events of yesterday and preparing for the trials today would bring.

Jenny Barnes is my favorite Wyandot County artist. One year at the county fair I told her about my walk to work. I said I thought that would make a wonderful painting. She agreed, but I knew she wasn't thrilled with the idea of doing paintings by commission. I took a picture of the scene one day and dropped it off at the office of Jim Barnes when I had my taxes done. (Jim is Jenny's husband. Wyandot County is a small place. You can get paintings and accounting done by the same family.)

More time passed. Still no word from Jenny. Then one day Gene Logsdon and I decided to publish a book together. What to do for a cover? How about, I suggested over lunch at Woody's Restaurant, the Breakfast In Carey painting?

The next day I called Jenny and she told me Gene (who also happens to be her brother) had already asked her to do the painting. She finally said yes to our request. And we're so glad she did. You now see the work on our cover. The original hangs in the office of The Progressor-Times.

Steve Zender

contents

contents

contents

dedication

This book is dedicated to those people who live in little places ... and to those who wish they did.

The big things
in life are
the little things

After casting about for some time, trying to find a name for our collection of columns, we had yet to find a title that satisfied us. Gene's suggestion of "It's a Small World" sounded too Disneyish to me, a thought that appalled The Country Rover.

I suggested "This Little World," which didn't excite either of us. And "Our Small World," we were afraid, would be misconstrued as being Logsdon's and Zender's world, rather than the world that belongs to all of us.

Then a book was loaned to me. It was "Hempfield," by Ray Stannard Baker, writing under the pseudonym of David Grayson. I will forever be indebted to Gene Logsdon for loaning me that book and to antiquarian book dealer Bob Hayman for finding it for Gene in the first place. "Hempfield" is a sort of love story. It involves a man and a woman, but it also involves a weekly newspaper, the people who produced it, and the town for which it was produced.

Gene and I both sort of fell in love with Anthy, the owner of The Star of Hempfield, and we both admired her father, a man whom the reader never meets. But Anthy's father is a character who quietly, without ever really being seen, permeates the entire story. He was the man who told his daughter, "The big things in life are the little things."

We hope our collection of columns, gleaned from past issues of The Carey Progressor and The Progressor-Times, with a couple of excerpts from Ohio Magazine thrown in, makes you laugh, cry and think. We don't claim anything here is equal to that 1915 masterpiece by David Grayson, but we do hope our writing continues to express the importance of little things in little places, for they so often are the big things in life.

Steve Zender

Life
in
little
places

The carving tree of life

Gene Logsdon
From July 12, 1989

Although less than half a mile away huge trucks groaned over the freeway and monster tractors belabored plowed fields, the time might as easily have been 1889, not 1989 in the woods where we walked. In the deep forest the old trees remembered Deunquat and Between-the-Logs, Crawford and Kenton, and old Nick Seifert showing a little boy, who would become my father, where he cached his food while he fished the Sandusky River. What stories trees might tell if only they could.

Sometimes they do tell stories. As we walked what seemed like a bit of lost wilderness, letting our feet take us where they would, we came to a beech tree with initials carved into its trunk. As I drew closer, my jaw dropped. The name carved there, now only barely readable, was mine! I would have sworn, a minute earlier, that I had never walked this particular place before. The initials of all the members of our family were also carved in the tree. The date: 1957. I shook my head in disbelief, but slowly, as my sister and I stretched our memories, the day, 32 years ago, came mistily back to us. Dad had taken the family for a picnic and while he fished and Mom

1

read, the rest of us had gone walking in the hills above the river.

What I kept thinking now was that we might easily have walked 20 feet to the left or to the right of that tree and never found it. Never found a lovely old memory kept sacred in a shrine of trees above the Sandusky River. What had guided our feet back to this spot in a trackless forest?

Gene Logsdon at the carving tree.

I am often conscious of how my life forever loops back upon itself, perhaps more so than is true of most people because of the peculiar circumstances of my life. We all pass through stages on the journey to the grave, and make friends and acquaintances of those we associate with at each stage: family, school, college, armed services perhaps, work or career, neighbors. Mostly we move on in our mobile, modern way, leaving the friends and acquaintances of one stage behind and making new friends in the next stage someplace else. But my life forever loops back, like crochet work, drawing bygone friends into my present.

The reason, I think, is that my stages have been more like brotherhoods: the brotherhood of boyhood; the brotherhood of seminary life; the brotherhood of family farming; the brotherhood of academic life; the brotherhood of writers – associations of deep emotional involvement.

I would never have believed, living in Philadelphia, that I would again look back into the lives of my grade school friends, and yet now scarcely a month goes by I do not see "Egger" or Don, and see the memories of a special long ago reflected in their eyes. All because I did what few people do anymore: I came home again.

But I did not in the process lose Philadelphia friends. Quite often my tracks cross with theirs because we are all bound together by our commitment to writing.

Nor have I lost college friends because my first college was unique: a seminary. A few years within the monastery-like confines of a Franciscan seminary effects a kinship closer than blood brothers. Last week there was a gathering of Franciscans at the shrine in Carey and one of them was kind enough to invite me to stop by. What a bittersweet feeling filled me. We all looked at each other with the same agonizing thought I'm sure: **How old and worn we had grown.**

The cruelty of that realization, blending with both splendidly funny and deeply sorrowful memories, evoked in me a strange, unsettling combination of fulfillment and loss that I can neither express properly or rid myself of. The heartstrings of life look back and bind my days into an ever-present now. I want to laugh and to cry at the same time. Old Heraclitus was wrong.

You can step into the same river twice. Sort of, anyway, if the river is a magical one, like the Sandusky.

3

Memories linger in the Pourhouse

Gene Logsdon
Feb. 19, 1986

A n Upper Sanduskian has to be really set in his ways to still refer to the Pourhouse restaurant on N. Sandusky Avenue as "Bolish's." But it was Bolish's for so long – the Bolish family operated it from 1900 to 1971 – that I can't get used to saying Pourhouse, which it became in the early '80s.

It doesn't smell quite like Bolish's did 40 years ago, thank God, but whenever I walk in there I am conscious of spirits out of the past hovering everywhere. Those old front tables used to sit in the back room where the longest euchre game in history was played. The players died and were replaced, but for over 60 years you could go back there any time of the day and watch the game in progress. "As a matter of fact it was still going on when we bought the place," says present owner Steve Morral with a good-natured grin. "When we scrubbed down those walls there must have been a quarter-inch of nicotine on them."

I can believe it. And I'll bet the plain wood floor that used to grace the place had an inch of dried tobacco juice on it. That's how I remember Bolish's. On the rare occasion my father took me in there with him when I was a boy, there were brass spittoons everywhere, and all those dirty, whiskery men (or so they seemed to me) tilting their heads back and sending brown streams of tobacco juice in the general direction of their dissatisfactions. Rarely ever did they hit the spittoons. "A former owner loaded those spittoons up – a whole pickup load – and dumped them in that fill behind the fairgrounds," Steve said sadly. I can see what archeologists a thousand years from now will say when they dig those brass relics up. "Urns," they will pronounce learnedly. "Probably used to offer incense to their gods." Which in a way I suppose is correct.

Anyhow, I was eating supper in the Pourhouse the other night on the very table that felt the almighty power of the right bower trumping the left bower for 70 years, when my eye chanced to fall upon a faded, sepia-toned photograph high on the wall. With a start I recognized in it the man whom I have long thought was only a product of my dreams. "He really existed," I blurted to my wife. "I didn't just make him up!" She rolled her eyes, used to such outbursts. In the photo, the man tending bar – the very bar behind which Steve Morral now stood – had no legs below the knees.

He walked on stubs that were encased in black, cylindrical shoeless boots that extended to his thighs. As a small child, I could hardly wait to get out of church on Sunday because of this man. After church, everyone gathered in little groups outside to talk awhile before going home. But I lurked silently in the shadow of my mother and waited for the man with no feet to walk down the church steps. The first time I saw him I jerked on Mom's hand and blurted: "Mommy, look at the man with stovepipes on his legs." She of course hushed my mouth in stern embarrassment, which only deepened the mystery for me. If she had said, "Oh, that's Joe Bolish and he got his legs cut off in a train accident," I would probably not have thought a whole lot more about it. But she didn't.

I concluded there must be something dreadfully evil about him. Every Sunday, far below the general level of conversation, I stared at the man's stovepipe boots to my heart's content. How fast could a person run in them? Were they made from stovepipe hats? Did it hurt to walk in them? Had his feet dropped off or just shrunk?

5

The big things in life are the little things

Then one Sunday he was gone and years later when I would think of him, I decided he was a product of dreams only. Now here he was, resurrected in a photograph. "That was Joe Bolish, the original owner of the bar," Morral said. "He lost his legs as the result of a train accident and used the money he collected from the settlement to buy this place." Later Theodore, his brother, bought Joe out and later his son, Ed, took over, who in turn sold the bar in 1971 to Tom Koehler. "It's unbelievable how profitable the place was in the early days," says Steve. "I found a bunch of old checks when we cleaned out the place. Our electric bill, for example, runs $500 to $600 a month. Then it was $17. The balance in just his check book was always between $12,000 and $20,000, and remember, that was in the days when a dollar was a real dollar."

My fondest memory of Bolish's was the veal and flank sandwiches. Village folklore says the sandwiches were not real veal but pork disguised as veal. But if that is true at all, I have a hunch it was true in the later years, not up into the 40s which is when I remember the sandwiches. You had a choice then of veal or flank (the latter was pork) and as a boy, my choice was veal. Nobody then or now, in the cheapest cafe or the finest restaurant from here to New York or Chicago, ever made a better sandwich to my taste. Maybe it was just because I so rarely ate one – rarely ate anything not fixed at home – that I favored them so. But the whole town loved them. My Aunt Helen Rall's eyes lit up when I mentioned Bolish's veal sandwiches the other day. She remembers them from earlier generations than mine. "Of course in **those** days," she says, "**we** weren't allowed into places like Bolish's. But we'd stand outside and beckon and the Bolish kids would serve us our sandwiches out on the sidewalk."

The big, carved wooden backdrop behind the bar at Bolish's, that is, the Pourhouse, has a longer history yet. "It was built in 1870 and stood in a hotel in Toledo until the Bolish brothers brought it here in 1900," says Morral. Artisans of great reputation often built these ornate bars and they are very much in demand today to put in new bars. "I've been offered $68,000 for this one," Morral says.

Above the bar sit bottles of prohibition wine, which Morral found in the basement when he cleaned it out. "Wine collectors say if it hasn't turned to vinegar, some of it can be quite valuable now. We tried some at New Year's. It was potent stuff."

Morral has sifted through some four or five feet of dirt under the sidewalk grate in front of the Pourhouse, finding coins, rings, and other curiosities from the past. "I quit at about five feet down although there is still another foot or so that ought to be sifted. The way I figured, when you get that far back in time, those old codgers who dropped a coin then would have thought enough of it to lift the grate and pick it up again."

Traders in antiques are always stopping by the Pourhouse, knowing Morral's interest in collectibles, especially anything connected with Budweiser beer. The strangest thing he has hung on the wall is an old helicopter propeller. "The guy wanted to sell me the whole helicopter," he says, "but I couldn't figure out how to get it in here."

"This place is also famous for having the oldest bartender in Ohio," says Helen Thiel, smiling from behind the bar. "That's me."

Mary and Joe Bolish

Bracing for the nostalgia

Steve Zender
May 11, 1994

This is the second week in our new home at 1198 E. Findlay Street.

Arne Hayman, the first employee at The Carey Progressor, was the last person to work at our old office. Arne admitted there was a little sadness connected with walking out of 109 W. Findlay Street for the final time. I haven't had that feeling yet but I've been sorting through 26 years of files so I'm bracing for a nostalgia attack.

Most interesting are the letters. There are all sorts of messages. Some people were telling me to turn to Jesus and others were telling me to go to hell.

Some were encouraging the newspaper to "tell it like it is." Others were saying we had already said way too much.

One letter which caused me to laugh out loud (I remember laughing the first time I read it, too) was challenging me to "have some guts and print this letter." The letter writer didn't have enough nerve to sign his name. So much for guts.

Most of the letters I found were nice, congratulatory in nature. I feel ashamed for not having acknowledged more of those letters than I have over the years. What a heel I've been. There was even a letter in 1969 from a journalism student named Star, whom I had met just once. Now if a single, 23-year-old male didn't reply to a girl named Star, just who would he write to?

M ost of the letters were connected with the business, but there were a few personal notes, too. For example, there was a note from an old Wittenberg classmate. We hadn't seen each other in more than 20 years but then had gotten together at Woody's. We drank too many martinis, rehashed the old days, laughed a lot, and had a good-natured argument or two. The letter was following up on my suggestion that we get together with our wives for dinner. That was six years ago and we haven't done it yet. Scott and his wife live so far away: Bucyrus, in the next county.

Another Wittenberg buddy, Tim Neher, had written to me long ago. I lost the letter, or so I had thought, and never replied. That was in 1975. I'm going to see if he still lives in Elyria.

Judy (I don't know her last name now) had written years ago, asking some advice for her job on a weekly newspaper. I still have the penciled reply I wrote. I was going to type it, but got busy. It's still there in my file.

There was also a nice letter from my cousin Hazel, telling me how much I've meant to her over the years. Have I ever thanked her for that? Thank you, Hazel.

And there were two notes from Ruth in Massachusetts. She works (worked?) for a reader service and it is, or was, her job to read newspapers for clients. Once we spelled Styrofoam without a capital s and later received a letter from Dow Chemical Company, telling us that Styrofoam is a brand name product of Dow and must always be capitalized. I wrote a column, wondering about the "spies" who were watching us. Ruth dropped me a note. She was that spy, she admitted.

Some time later my mother returned one of our reader questionnaires. Mom didn't sign her name, but in the "comments" section she noted that she loved the paper and that, while she hadn't read every weekly paper in the state, it surely must be one of the best. "Of course, I might be prejudiced," she added, "since I'm your mom." Shortly after my mother's note, I received another note from Ruth in Massachusetts. "Your mother is absolutely right!" she wrote. "Your paper is one of the best weekly papers in the state. But I can go her one better. I **have** read every weekly in the state!" She signed it, "Your favorite spy?" No doubt. Thank you, Ruth from Massachusetts. And thank you, Mom.

There were a couple of letters from Esther Leathers, the English teacher. If you graduated from Carey High School in my era, you say her name reverently. She's dead now. Why didn't I ever tell her how much those little notes of encouragement meant to me?

I found all sorts of items as I sorted through the old files: Money from readers (along with some very funny letters) responding to my bogus pleas for money, in the spirit of Oral Roberts and other evangelists. There were several letters in response to my Young, Unhurried, Country Citizens (Yuccie) proposal, and copies of letters I had written, including one to an Upper Sandusky lawyer and another to Jimmy Buffett. Neither, by the way, replied.

There were even a couple of nice notes from people who have often been harsh critics.

I like our new place. I think it will be a nice place for all of us to work and I think it will make our newspaper more efficient. We've seen quite a few changes – most for the better – since we opened that first Progressor office in the spot where Clair Shane's barbershop is now located. And to Tim and Mary and John and Hazel and Peggy and Ruth and Scott and Ann and Star and all the others, I'm sorry I didn't write. Here's hoping our move has taught me one important lesson: Value the opinion of others . . . and answer your mail.

A happy cry

Steve Zender
July 10, 1996

The first time Molly cried in front of Patty Loveless, it was as a member of a crowd in Toledo. This time, it was face-to-face and arm-in-arm with her hero.

The first time was sad. This time was happy. "I'd never had a happy cry," Molly told me later.

I would imagine it will be awhile before the two of us experience a more memorable weekend.

It was our first trip to the Country Concert at Hickory Hill Lake in Fort Loramie. Thousands of country music fans pack the place every year to hear an astounding array of singers, from hot young stars like Tim McGraw and Faith Hill, to country legend George Jones.

The squeamish need not attend. The place is awash with beer and squirt-bottle-equipped, partially-clad crazies. But these people love their country music. It's a rowdy but happy crowd. It's great.

The big things in life are the little things

My family has seen Patty Loveless in concert many times, with Molly and her dad slightly bigger Loveless Lunatics than the others. I figure if there are Kentucky angels in heaven, they sing a lot like Patty Loveless. And if I'm honest, I suspect they even look a little like her.

Patty Loveless is from Pikeville, Ky. Carey has a large number of residents from that part of eastern Kentucky and I'd like to write a story - from a small-town perspective - about this woman, daughter of a coal miner, who knew as a youngster she wanted to sing that uniquely American music we call country. I picture a story with a correlation between her experience and the folks who followed U.S. 23 to places like Carey, Ohio, and made a good life for themselves.

But on this day, the emphasis wasn't on writing a story, it was on hearing our favorite singer and maybe getting an autograph.

Patty Loveless usually sings about love. Good love, bad love, young love and old love. Broken, bent, fixed and finished love. She crosses some sort of invisible line between blue grass music of the Appalachian hills and good old rock and roll. She sometimes sings happy and, dear God, can she sing sad.

The crying in Toledo came when the singer had trouble finishing one of her most noted songs, "How Can I Help You Say Goodbye." Fans, who gave her a standing ovation upon completion of the number, discovered later the singer had just been informed that day of a sister's hospitalization. Her sister died weeks later. Patty did not sing "How Can I Help You Say Goodbye" at Hickory Hill Lake.

At Hickory Hill, the travelling equipment of the various stars rolls in and out throughout the day and it was quite by accident that Molly caught a glimpse of the purple bus pulling into the lot.

Wearing a Patty Loveless T-shirt from a previous concert and holding the brand new one she had just purchased, Molly was standing alone beside an access road, waving, when the bus rolled in. "I saw Patty waving at me," Molly claimed, but I was skeptical. That tinted glass could play tricks on the mind of a true believer.

Molly had her fan club card at the ready as we checked with security people to see if club members would get to meet with the star. They didn't think so. Later in the day, we asked a member of Patty's staff if he would deliver a gift and we sent a Young, Unhurried County Citizen shirt and membership card and letter. (The Yuccies are explained elsewhere in this book.) We watched as her bus door swung open and the gift was delivered to someone inside.

We returned after Patty's performance to check out the fan club situation. No, there wasn't going to be any "meet and greet," as they call it in the business. But then a strange, wonderful thing happened.

As groups of people gawked, trying to get a look at Patty or any of the other popular acts that were there, a young man walked over to us and said, "You two come with me."

We dutifully obliged, following him around the buses to where a security guard stood, making sure any well-wishers went no farther. We were told to walk between two of the buses, just the two of us, and there she

Molly Zender and Patty Loveless

stood. Patty Loveless. Smiling. Alone, near the door of her bus.

"Oh my God," Molly said as we walked down the narrow corridor between the buses. And she began to cry. Molly never did express the slightest bit of embarrassment over her emotional outburst, but Patty had a genuine look of concern as Molly sobbed. "I didn't mean to make you cry," she said. She put her arm around Molly's shoulder and later suggested I wait "until those tears dry," before taking a picture.

I don't even remember telling the woman how much we loved her music, but then she already knew that. I asked if she had received our gift and was impressed that she remembered the T-shirt was green. She hadn't had time to read the letter, she said, but promised to do so.

She said, "Turn around here baby," when she put the new T-shirt on Molly's back to autograph it, and drew Molly close to her when I took a picture. "I saw you wavin' at me when we came in," she later told Molly.

I suppose we could have stayed longer, got autographs on more items, asked more questions, taken more pictures, but we didn't want to overstay our welcome. It wasn't long after we left and headed back to the concert that we saw the purple vehicle heading off toward the next town.

We stopped for a Pepsi for Molly (the only soft drink served at the concert) and an Old Milwaukee for me (the only beer served). The guy who waited on us plopped down the drinks and said, "There you go, a Budweiser and a 7-Up."

"We don't care what you give us," I said. "Molly and I just met Patty Loveless."

"Is she your hero, Molly?" the man asked. Molly said yes. "It's good to have heroes," the man observed.

We're still amazed at our good fortune. It sometimes pays to be patient and persistent. Molly said she prayed too. Maybe there was a Kentucky angel listening, one who understands that sad cries are sometimes important, but happy cries are even better.

A traditional hog butchering

Gene Logsdon
Dec. 15, 1982

WWalking into Dave Pahl's barnyard south of Kirby on the day after Thanksgiving is like walking back into childhood. It's a tradition in the Pahl family to butcher hogs the two days after Thanksgiving when the weather is usually just right for cooling the meat but not yet too cold to freeze it. The hogs are processed using the ways that have proven themselves for centuries. The only new tools are an electric bandsaw and an electric slicer to cut up the meat.

Wood blazed beneath four big black kettles steaming with boiling water in the center of the barnyard. On a trailer bed next to the barn, a group of sturdy young men scalded dead hogs and scraped off the hair with old-fashioned hog scrapers. Another group of young men brought newly-killed hogs to the scalding barrel. The cleanly scraped carcasses were moved on to the scaffolds, hung up, gutted and split by an older group of men.

Everyone had his or her job. As each carcass was opened on the scaffold, the entrails were carefully gathered in pans and carried to the building Dave has renovated and equipped for butchering. There the women begin the onerous task of cleaning the intestinal casings which will become the skin for the stuffed sausage. Despite women's lib, this job is always done by women, probably because it doesn't take great physical strength, but lots of intestinal fortitude (no pun intended) which I have always noticed women possess more of than men.

Meanwhile the men who, for reasons of age or infirmity, can't heave the heavy hog carcasses around, begin the tedious work of cutting the meaty parts of the hog heads from the skulls. Some of this meat is used to make what the Pahls call "swagamauger." No one knows how that word is spelled. The hog's stomach is cleaned out, the head meat put into the lining, the lining tied closed, and the meat smoked. Later it will be sliced and eaten. That's swagamauger. Smoked headcheese might be a rough translation. Although the Pahls do not make blood pudding and don't put the ears in the headcheese, very little of anything else is wasted. "We make use of everything but the squeal," says Dave.

The traditional meal on butchering day is fresh tenderloin, the best meat in the world in my estimation. Sweetbreads (the thymus gland) and brains are also part of that meal – for those who like this meat.

On the second day of a Pahl butchering, the meat is cut up into hams, shoulders, ribs, bacon, hocks and chops. Down both sides of a long table in the butcher shop men and women bend to the task. Those who know their meatcutting skills do the major surgery, the less skilled cutting trimmings into lard fat and sausage meat. The lard fat is further divided into the lean fat or internal fat and the exterior back fat. The former cooks down quicker than the latter and the two must not be put into the rendering kettle at the same time.

The work moves along with a marvelous efficiency, everyone knowing his or her job. The finer cuts, as for the pork chops, are done on the bandsaw. The bacon is sliced on an electric slicer. The sausage meat is spread out on another table in batches, salted, peppered and then ground. Rosy Pahl, Dave's wife, fries a couple of patties of the first grinding for all to taste to make sure the salt and pepper content is just right. After the sausage is ground, it goes into the stuffer which squeezes it into the casings. Meanwhile, the fat, cut into small pieces, goes back outside into the big lard kettle over the roaring fire. The grease cooks out as the fat is stirred constantly with long wooden paddles to keep it from burning.

A traditional hog butchering

When the fat is all cooked down, it and the grease are poured into the lard press, where the last of the grease is squeezed out. That leaves the "cracklins" which taste like delicious potato chips until you eat one too many. The grease is poured into crocks where it hardens into pure white lard. "You can't buy decent lard anymore," someone remarks. Says another, "You can't buy lard at all some times." A third remarks, "You can always use Crisco." Everyone snickers. Country people know that a pie without a lard crust is no pie at all.

The traditional meal on the second day of butchering at the Pahls is fresh sausage. And oh, so good. Doubly good to my taste because the Pahls don't use spices in their sausage. Who needs spices for meat so good? There is a lard crust apple pie to round off the meal.

Over the entire butchering, Grandma (Mrs. Agnes Pahl) reigns with a steady, efficient hand. She is a marvel, cleaning guts, grinding sausage, feeding casings onto the stuffed sausage, helping wherever help is needed. I asked her how many hogs she has butchered in her lifetime. "About 10 a year," she said. "And how many years would that be?" I asked. Her eyes twinkled. "Now that would be tellin', wouldn't it?" She did admit, however, to being married 60 years, so I figured she's butchered at least 600 hogs and cleaned well over a mile of sausage casings. On her farm just outside Carey,

Hog butchering at Dave Pahl's place

17

she raises a few hogs herself, and lots of other things, including peacocks.

Butchering is hard, unpleasant work for the most part. But when family and friends get together, many hands make light the task, as the old saying goes, and there is a sort of festive spirit to the work. "You raise your own meat, you do your own butchering, you save some money," sums up Dave Pahl. "And when you do it this way, there's a little fun, too."

Dave and Rosy Pahl are as modern and up-to-date as they need to be, but they cherish the old ways. The kids on butchering day learn a thing or two about feeding themselves and a whole lot more about the fact that you get out of life what you put into it. If you want to eat fresh tenderloin, you by hickory got to work for it.

Maggie was a good old dog

Steve Zender
April 10, 1996

Our old dog died last summer. We sure miss that dog, but let's set the record straight, right at the start. Intelligence wasn't the old cocker spaniel's strong suit. But then I never figured brainpower was the best measure of worth anyway, whether it was in man or beast. We never planned on winning awards with Maggie. We just loved her.

Her registered name was Maggie O'Zee because she was born on St. Patrick's Day. She was my birthday gift to my wife and the present was a surprise, even to our daughters. I can still see it plain as day. Sue and the three girls were all in the kitchen when I set the furry little blond bundle down in the middle of the floor. Molly, just over a year old at the time, grinned in awe while Amy and Sarah jumped up and down and shouted with glee, scaring the already frightened little pup half to death.

Little did I know how many hours I would be investing in that birthday gift. "Bathroom duty" remained my responsibility throughout the animal's life. I credit Maggie with helping me get to know the constellations better. I did plenty of gazing into the heavens at night . . . waiting.

The big things in life are the little things

I bought the dog on a Wednesday, after playing golf. Rick Miller went with me to pick her up. Rick was so enamored of the pups that he bought one of Maggie's sisters on the spot. We got the dogs mixed up on the way home, so I'll never know if Maggie was the animal I chose or the one Rick picked out. The thought never crossed my mind at the time that this little puppy would out-live my good friend.

Maggie

Maggie would "sit" when she was told and that was about her entire repertoire of "tricks." But she didn't need to jump through hoops to make us happy.

You couldn't have hoped for a more pleasant personality than Maggie's. That's not to say there weren't problems from time to time. She wouldn't allow police chief Bill Swartz, a lover of dogs if there ever was one, in our house once. And then there was the time the ever-hungry animal consumed an entire bowl of grease. I came home to a house with everyone in bed, including the dog. But before she had retired, Maggie had deposited piles of regurgitated grease throughout the house. It resembled that plastic fake vomit you might have seen. I tracked her through the kitchen into the living room and up the steps to Molly's bedroom, where she lay. Sick as a dog.

So was I after cleaning up the mess. Maggie lived through that one, but barely. Her coat was shiny, but she didn't move much for several days.

Her near-death-experience with grease didn't kill her appetite for food. The floors would always be clean as long as Maggie was around. And, as irritating as her begging could sometimes become, that sad, soulful look, with the head cocked to one side, worked more often than not.

She would usually wait impatiently to be fed. But the time she decided to help herself to the Italian sub I held in my hand led to another near-death-experience. Luckily – for both of us I suppose – Maggie escaped behind the couch until my anger subsided. The kids will tell you I tried to kill her, but they know better.

Maggie loved her home, but she would occasionally take off exploring. I would swear I'd never look for her again, but we'd end up scouring the neighborhood, often finding the dog across Spring Run, eating bread the Twinings had put out for the birds. We had a difficult time scolding her because we were too happy at finding her.

Maggie chased birds, rabbits and cats, but wasn't a hunter. Unless hunting for food counted.

A couple of her descendants are still around town but our attempts at raising cocker spaniels weren't very successful. Only two puppies survived in her first litter and none in her second. We decided there should be no more attempts at motherhood.

Maggie aged gracefully, growing gray but staying in relatively good health. I grew a little gray myself during the time she was with us. The kids grew up. Time marched on. Then one day last summer, with Molly, her best buddy, by her side, Maggie jumped up, gave a short whimper, and died. We rushed her to the veterinarian, but Maggie was dead of a heart attack. She was 13.

All of us grieved. Later we called Amy in Toledo with the bad news. Sarah, by ironic coincidence, phoned from work during her break, at the very moment the dog fell to the floor, dead. I excitedly told her we were on our way to the vet. Later we had to call her back at work to tell her the dreadful news. When we drove to my parents' house to inform them of the tragedy, it was like reporting the death of a friend.

I buried Maggie that night in a driving rain storm. As the thunder crashed about me and the rain ran down my nose, I figured my family might have to throw me in there beside the old girl if one of those lightning bolts went astray.

Maggie is mentioned often in our house. We still expect to be greeted by her when we arrive home. A certain chair is still her chair. When Amy brings her cat home, we chuckle at how Maris drove poor old Maggie crazy, standing on the foot stool and batting the dog in the head as she walked by. March 17 is still St. Patrick's Day, but it also remains Maggie's birthday.

We have our own cat in residence now. Nellie, a gift to Sarah, was added to another long list of females at our house to out-number me – wife, daughters, dog, (fish?). Or so we thought.

We took Nellie to Dr. Wenner to be spayed. "What's your cat's name?" he asked when we stopped back to pick her up after the "operation." "Nellie," he was told. "You might want to change it," he suggested. Nellie was actually a boy and became Nelson from that point on.

If cats can have a personality, Nelson has a good one. He's goofy and he's good company. But nothing will ever replace that dumb old dog.

Wharton's favorite game

Gene Logsdon
Oct. 22, 1986

If someone would have asked me a month ago if there were a genuine, professional, sand-tamped croquet court in Wyandot County I'd have laughed at the preposterousness of the question. I thought croquet was serious business in Victorian England with maybe the last vestiges of it lingering on the grand lawns of old mansions in the South. But in Wharton? Yep. In Wharton. And not one court, but two.

More amazing yet, at least to me, is that croquet has been a serious sport in Wharton for at least 100 years. Wayne Cole remembers playing 56 years ago, and since there were old avid players even then, we can only speculate how far back adults were playing the game in an organized way. Wayne remembers a court behind a house across the street from the school, then one behind the hardware store, and finally one beside Sam Corbin's garage, which was in use in the '50s. Glenn Frank says he has heard there was a court at one time behind the bank.

Jack Opper is the town's most avid player today, and the game's most enthusiastic proponent. "When I was a child, 50 years ago, I was allowed to watch the oldtimers play. I learned to love the game then. There is so much strategy in croquet that I'm just fascinated by it."

When World War II came along, the young players went away to war and the old ones gradually died off. Croquet lapsed for awhile, only to be revived in the '50s. It simmered down again in the '70s, and now with the court in the park, interest is high again. If you should see the night sky lit up over Wharton some summer night way past midnight, it's the lights from the croquet court. Games have been known to last into the wee hours.

The courts are 72 feet long and 35 feet wide, about a foot of gravel deep and sand tamped down on top. Opper laid out the courts and worked up the rules from the memories of old time Wharton players and the encyclopedia. "We follow the rules of regulation play mostly, but with some of our own variations," he says. The sand court is traditional, even though in highbrow croquet, the court is grass much like a golf green. In Wharton a hundred years ago there was no way to build a manicured green.

The mallets the Wharton players use are unique to Wharton and better than the ones featured recently in "Fine Woodworking" magazine. Bob Coakley, a retired sheet metal worker and avid croquet player, makes them in his Wharton shop. The handles are much shorter than on the clubs you buy for backyard games. You have to stoop way over to use them. Coakley's handles are usually of ash, and the mallets of maple or oak. He turns the mallets down on his lathe to the precise micron desired, then slips a heated stainless steel ring (cut from an exhaust pipe) over each end. As the steel cools, it shrinks irrevocably tight against the wood. "Well, I didn't really have to learn how to do that," says Bob. "When I was a kid in Carey, I watched my grandfather (Emmanuel Drummond) shrink steel rims on wagon wheels in his blacksmith shop."

That finished, Coakley adds the touch that makes his mallets different and better than any other. He puts a strike plate of aluminum over each end, making it almost impossible for the wood to splinter. A Coakley mallet should last a few days after forever. Glenn Frank, who lives a few miles east of Wharton and who has made mallets for local players too, says the preferred wood is oak from an old barn beam. "It's a wonder all the old barns around here aren't falling down," he jokes. "Those croquet players keep removing the beams to make into mallets."

The big things in life are the little things

Croquet is not a boring game, as I had thought. Not the way the serious players play it. The game combines the precision of billiards, the strategy of chess and the tense pressure of golf. So complex is the strategy of positioning balls both offensively and defensively that a rule has been put into effect allowing no more than two minutes between shots to keep partners from discussing all their alternative moves too long.

I'm not yet sure croquet is a game for softball players, however. Whenever I shot and missed, out of my mouth came the same words I use when I hit into a double play. Unlike golf, you can chatter while the other player eyes up his ball preparatory to shooting, but expletives are frowned on. Nor would anyone dream of shouting at a referee or throwing his mallet in disgust. Croquet may not only be too intelligent for softball players but too civilized.

There remains, however, a mystery. Why has croquet been so traditional as an adult game in the Wharton area and seemingly nowhere else locally? Were there courts in other towns? Did Carey or Sycamore or Upper Sandusky ever have a croquet court? How early was the game played here? Which ethnic group, if any, introduced the game? It appears from history the game came from England by way of Europe and then to New England, and thence to the midwest. Was there an influential Yankee family in early Wharton? Love to know.

Community life is alive and well in Sycamore

Gene Logsdon
Nov. 7, 1990

Ilove little villages because they are the most genuine repository of that indefinable thing we call a sense of community. Many people, in fact most people, no longer live within a real community, and that is why you hear urban and suburban society talk so much about a loss of identity. They try to make up for their lack of community by joining a club, or a special interest group, or by continuous hobnobbing with a closed circle of friends. Motorcycle gangs, religious orders, the Cleveland Browns' Dog Pound, the DAR, the Farm Bureau, the Rotarians. They are all substitutes for real community, or are only parts of real community.

Clubs and circles of friends are not community because they are exclusionary. They do not represent a true cross section of society, nor do they share a common binding economic interest. A real community includes within it all the occupational groups necessary for a society to function, and is small enough so that everyone is aware of a common economic interest. Some of the people may despise each other, but they know they have to join in mutual cooperation if they are to survive.

The big things in life are the little things

It is difficult to achieve this kind of commonality in cities or even medium-sized towns because the human mind just can't grasp the interconnectedness of true economy in such large groups. For example, if you live in New York City, you may never see a cow or a field of corn in your life and so you are not likely to worry much about farmers going broke. Likewise, if you are a sheepherder on a 50,000-acre Montana ranch, you will have a hard time getting interested in whether a Detroit autoworker makes a living or not. The very complexity of the term "modern society" causes the mind to grow weary of the big picture, and to retreat into clubs and groups and special causes and friendships.

You can retreat from real community in a village too, of course, but it is very difficult. In Carey or Sycamore, you are going to run into representatives of almost all walks of life over a year's time if you do anything at all besides watch TV. You can't hide in the exclusive retreat of the guarded suburban enclave, or a well-heeled country club. If you are poor, you can't hide in a ghetto. Either rich or poor you can't escape the retarded and the unwed mothers and the religious fanatics and the secular humanists. They are going to be within walking distance of you. Villagers are forced to deal with the real world, and that is why they should be the most well-rounded and knowledgeable people in society

Real community is when you hear a car dealer say that he watches the crops as fervently as the farmers do because if the corn is poor, car sales will be poor too. Real community is feeling concern when a good man loses his job, even in a totally unrelated business, because you know good men are hard to find. I saw a person turn in a $100 bill she found under a restaurant table recently, and then the whole restaurant staff worried until they figured out who had last been seated at that table. That's what a sense of community does for society.

I was thinking about all that while I was enjoying a pleasant experience in Sycamore over the last two months, playing in the over-35 softball league. Where else would one find a big iron kettle of stew over a fire, prepared for the players and spectators? What was really amusing was that, typical of the ingenuity of rural villagers, the kettle was suspended over the fire from a hydraulic manure scoop on an old International Harvester tractor.

There was something special in the air – besides the smell of that stew. First of all, with all the sports hullabaloo that goes on everywhere over everything, Sycamore has never been rightfully honored as one of the hottest places in Ohio for softball, especially fast pitch. Having grown up playing fast pitch in Upper Sandusky, I used to groan when Sycamore was coming to town because I knew we were going to get beat.

I guess it started with the Bogard family. I don't know how genetics manages all this, but Bogards are born with an ability to throw a softball underhanded fast enough to kill mosquitoes in flight. There were lots of other good players too, including a fellow by the name of Warnement who died right on the playing field, and to whom Sycamore erected a monument at the ball park. When Upper's Payne Realty battled all the way to the National Class A fast pitch tourney (about a decade ago), to be beaten finally by a team from California, a lot of the key players were from Sycamore.

So here we all were, softball diehards over 35, playing one more tournament, some of us wondering if it would be our last. Willy Rettig was there, playing still, and confessed that he would soon be 68. Rex Hankins was there, the two of us swapping stories from now to way back, he being one of the star players on that Payne Realty team, and still the manager of the Sycamore fast pitch team. Rex finally dropped out of the tournament on Saturday with pulled muscles in both legs, but before that he showed he could still rip a line drive to right field like he's done for what seems like a hundred years.

I had never before really gotten to know Sycamore, it being at the opposite end of the county from my usual haunts. I met some very nice people, all having a good time. During a game I might get razzed for an error on the field or an error I'd committed in print, but it all came out in a wonderfully friendly way. Between games there was lots of talk – wonderful community talk about jobs, about local politics, about school problems, about the Mideast, about some very funny stories.

I say I love softball because of the camaraderie, but it really is a sense of community I feel on occasions like this. I think you will meet every occupational group, age level, income, politics, religion and education in a village softball league, just as you will on a village street.

Things don't really change much after all

Gene Logsdon
July 11, 1990

One of the errors I often make as a journalist is to overestimate the speed of change. Or to conclude that a particular change is permanent. For example, I thought by now that organized Christianity in America would be on the wane, but in some ways it is stronger than ever.

I get paid for spotting trends and writing about them because that's what people want to read, or at least that's what magazines want to publish. But the danger of being "out in front" is that the majority situation never catches up with the "out-in-front" position, or by the time the mainstream does catch up, the "new" age is back to where the mainstream was originally. Whatever goes around, comes around, as we say.

Last Sunday my wife and I took a little drive around the neighborhood to see how the crops were doing and get an ice cream cone in Harpster. "This is what we always did 50 years ago!" I suddenly exclaimed. What was surprising is that we met, along the way, three other families doing the same thing. Everything that goes around, comes around.

Fifty years ago, driving out to view the neighbors' crops and stopping along the way for an ice cream cone was a summer evening ritual. My parents usually stopped at Spook's Tavern for ice cream because it was less than a mile away. But we might get as far as Harpster, or stop at Roger's grocery (Southside now) on the edge of Upper Sandusky, or at Little Sandusky, or even the grocery store at Brownstown, which Dillinger held up. There was also a store between Upper and Little Sandusky on old 23 that we frequented, and I don't mean Rieser's, which came later. In the countryside of the '30s and '40s, you were never more than a mile from an ice cream cone.

Sure, times have changed since then. But we are still scarcely ever more than five miles from an ice cream cone, and considering the difference between a buggy and a 1990 Cougar, I'd say that's remarkable. By **logical** deduction, looking only at transportation, we should have to drive maybe 25 miles to buy an ice cream cone.

I remember 50 years ago viewing crops from the back seat of a '37 Ford. That car would go in excess of 85 mph, and it got better mileage than cars today without all the modern folderol, so I question whether we have really changed much in automobiles – they all still have four wheels, I think. At least you can view the crops from a '37 vintage car just as well as from a '90 car.

As for the ice cream, I think it tasted better, if anything, in 1937 than it does today, but that might be because I hungered for it more then. There's a kind of slickness in ice cream today – gelatin, I think – that makes the chocolate and the butter pecan and the strawberry all taste more alike than different. But to balance that, there are more flavors today.

Nor has there been much change in the crops. Oh, the fields are bigger in some cases, and you don't see as much oats, and the corn and wheat aren't as tall as they used to be, but except for canola, we're growing the same plants. And some of the wet holes are still where they always were, despite a century of "scientific tile drainage." In wet, difficult springs like this one, the same fields that looked like hell in wet difficult springs of the '40s look like hell in 1990 too. And to a remarkable degree, the same farm families which grew good crops in spite of it in 1940 still grow good crops in spite of it in 1990.

The non-changing characteristics of fields I have known for 50 years are amazing, and so is the stubbornness of the farmers who plant them. There are wet holes in Wyandot County that have been plowed for more than 50 years, but have produced a crop only about five times. Yet the farmers try to farm them every year with a kind of optimism that you find elsewhere only in mental homes. There is no telling how many thousands of dollars of seed corn and fertilizer and herbicide have been squandered in this way. These wet holes were meant by nature to be cranberry bogs or duck ponds or frog holes, and if the farmers would have scooped them out a little more and made lakes out of them, they would have made far more money selling fishing fees. And done the environment a lot more good, too.

Nor has the countryside through which we drive while viewing the crops really changed much. The Tymochtee is still where it always was, and those little bottoms along it are still flooding out year after year like they always did, only now farmers have found a way to make flooding pay. They put these acres in various government programs and the stupid bureaucrats pay them our money for not getting a crop off of them. (Yeah, who's really the stupid one?) If the landowners had planted these bottoms to black walnut trees 50 years ago, they might be rich now and the tax money paid out for lost grain crops could have been used for some other useless purpose.

The wildlife, if anything, is more abundant now than it was 50 years ago. The rabid environmentalists who are always weeping for the lost wildlife should drive through our countryside these days. Be careful or a deer will run into you. The woodchucks sit along the road, one every 50 feet, like the bears do in Yellowstone, waiting for a handout. The coons are stealing more pet food out of barns than the pets are eating. I would not be surprised if the pet food industry were not the leading lobby for shorter coon hunting seasons. And for every chicken Wyandot County has lost to the big chicken factories, 3,000 geese have moved in to take its place.

There was a time when watching the trends of the '60s and '70s, I would have said that the countryside where I have viewed crops for 50 years would be empty of houses altogether, just as I thought the churches would be empty of people. No way. Some of the old houses have fallen down or been pulled down, but to balance that, many new ones have been built or old ones rebuilt. You find them tucked away everywhere in the countryside and I have a hunch this is the real new age coming along, not the expensive city suburb which I fear is so overpriced that it is due for a collapse.

All the new people making homes in the country are why I think there will be a school again in Harpster, if not Mifflin. If there is an ice cream cone waiting for us every five miles, can a school be far behind?

Going in social circles

Gene Logsdon
Nov. 11, 1987

The whirlwinds of high society have nothing on Wyandot County. There's so much to do anymore, I'm going to have to learn how to change clothes faster. Halloween weekend the schedule got so jammed for some families the only way to get to all of the scheduled events was to split up – wife to one, husband to another.

By following a strict schedule of only staying 1.3 hours at each gala affair, the two could attend an art show in Columbus, dine at Woody's, watch Upper Sandusky get beat again in football, compete in an archery contest, attend the concert at Tiffin's Ritz Theater, remember times past at the 10th anniversary celebration at the newly-decorated Star Theatre in Upper, feast on scrumptious roast hog at my brother's farm, and get in some square dancing at Justin Hollanshead's harvest party at the ancestral Hollanshead farmstead. I dare Bill Buckley and his fast lane to top that. In fact, what we need in this county are some faster country roads, so we can get around quicker.

The big things in life are the little things

But otherwise, technology is doing its darndest to make sure we miss nothing. While we are out, the VCRs record what's on in the rest of the world so we can see it later. Although at the rate things are going, later will never come. There's a restaurant in Columbus, I hear, that has three huge wall-to-wall screens so you can watch three different sports activities at once. But who has time to watch sports?

I got to the hog roast, the harvest dance and the 10th anniversary celebration at the Star. All first rate, and poignantly nostalgic for us older-timers. Highlight of the evening at the Star was a film of earlier days in Upper Sandusky that made me cry and laugh at the same time. Phyllis Beausay Ryerse put the movie together from the footage shot by her father Lanne Beausay and Buss Olpp back in the '30s and '40s, along with some takes of modern Upper Sandusky and residents today. A little sad to see old buddies like Don Dannenhauer looking forlorn in a pair of short pants in grade school. As they say, it seems like only yesterday. You can buy a copy of the tape for $30. Contact the Star Players.

The Star has been refurbished with new seats and aisle runners and redecorated. The community spirit that breathes so vitally in the activities of the Star is a continuing source of inspiration. I know I sound like a broken record, but I can promise you that if you get involved in a stage production, the emotional and even spiritual satisfaction you will derive from it beats most vacation thrills, plus the fact that you will form enduring relationships with the other people involved in the production. It is a great way to revitalize your zest for life.

The new parts of the film about Upper gave some close looks at our courthouse, making the point that the building is quite unusual and ornate. All these years I had taken it for granted and never noticed those stained glass windows at all. If that building were in Greece, and we saw pictures of it in some glossy travel magazine, we'd all ooh and aah over it. But since it is part of our growing up, we take it for granted. The film also made me realize that we could not afford to build that courthouse today. If we have had so much progress, and if the standard of living has advanced so much, why can't we build that way today? Somebody tell me.

It reminds me of another strange but true observation. Our township schools were built back between 1910 and 1920 mostly, and even though they have been allowed to deteriorate because the available money had to go for increased teacher salaries, they are still in better structural shape than that stupid flat-roofed monster of a senior high school in Upper which is not 30 years old. There must be a lesson there someplace.

Another interesting thing about the film was a brief take of Jeff Roth answering the question about why he liked Upper Sandusky. Jeff said when he was young, all he could think about was getting away. But after a few years of the big city, Upper looked mighty nice to him.

I second the motion. After 10 years in Philadelphia, one thing I know for sure – small villages are far, far better places to live than any city. Not everyone feels that way, and so we all gravitate to the kind of place that suits us best. Most of us love our hometown because our roots are here, but some of us have had a chance to compare, and roots or no roots, we made a deliberate choice: small is better than large. That's why I argue so hard when I hear some well-intentioned individual talking big about lots of growth, as if that were the greatest thing in the world. You want lots of growth, go live in a city, I say. You make a choice. You want a lot of money that growth gives to the few, go someplace that growth is already spoiling.

If I never had to leave Wyandot County again, I'd be perfectly satisfied. I've been enough places to know that what really counts in life is not a change of scene or a bunch of money but good friends, good food, and decent elbow room – no crowds, no traffic jams, a population mostly of common-sensed, ordinary people. The fall colors in Wyandot County are just as beautiful as they are in New England, just in smaller amounts. And the folks at Justin's barn dance and at Giles' hog roast were having every bit as much fun as the high societies of New York and San Francisco – with a lot shorter drive home.

Do the "operators" ever take the "risk" any more?

Steve Zender
Oct. 23, 1996

I'm wondering how many business people know the definition of "Entrepreneur:" "A person who organizes, operates and **assumes the risk for** a business venture."

Unfortunately, we seem to be seeing more and more people who are real "operators" but fewer and fewer who want to be "risk takers."

A fellow named Wilson Harrell recently wrote a column which declared: "Move to the future. Entrepreneurs are migrating to America's small towns and loving it." Since I've been singing the praises of small towns like Carey, Ohio, most of my life, I am delighted that others are beginning to see the benefits little communities have to offer, both for raising a family and owning a business. Mr. Harrell was telling business people to "go out among the rednecks and the gentlefolks" and I wanted to shout approval. But there was something troubling about the tone of his article.

Mr. Harrell told about his friend John who had moved his business (he didn't say what it was) from Washington, D.C., to a little town two hours away. The town had one red light, Mr. Harrell noted, and John already

34

seemed to know everyone in his small community.

Mr. Harrell talked about the deal John had gotten on a home he was going to renovate; the horse stable he was going to build; the dog kennel and the putting green he had planned.

The columnist urged businesses to "Go where it's fresh, out where rednecks and gentlefolks still believe that 'family values' are an assumed way of life, not a political slogan."

He said the movement to small towns and villages is a revolution, exclaiming, "Long live the revolution."

I enjoyed the bragging-up of small towns. But there were nagging questions.

After talking about John's 50 acres of land, the home, the stable, the kennels and the putting green, Mr. Harrell then mentions "the deal he had cut" with the town fathers regarding his business.

What kind of deal?

As a native of a small town and a business person who vigorously tries to avoid "cutting deals," I found Mr. Harrell's choice of words disturbing. Cutting deals? Just what does that mean?

Small towns, to my way of thinking, are charming in their own right. Yes, business can be good for a community. It can provide leadership, jobs, tax money. Good businesses can lift up a community and make it a better place. But business can also cause problems: pressures on the schools, the streets, the sewers, the water system. Growth, if small towns are not cautious and wise, can cause difficulties that residents were trying to avoid in the first place. Community leaders must remember that most small-town residents are living there by choice! They didn't move to a small community, hoping it would grow to Gotham.

All of Wyandot County has less than 25,000 people living in it and we are ripe for the picking if our governmental leaders want to "cut deals."

Already our county is watching a mountain grow in the flatlands of Crawford Township as garbage is hauled to our landfill from across the state and the country. Carey has had more than its share of air pollution for years, thanks to a lime plant, and now it must contend with a stench caused by two lime pelletizing plants. The county is dealing with the problems produced by giant hog farms. Egg "factories," involving millions of chickens, are proposed for two sites nearby and the tales of pollution and labor violations from the company involved frighten most citizens.

But some businesses like the little places because land is cheap, expenses are low, and the government has tended to look favorably on business and askance at those without political clout. Residents of Sycamore have millions of tires stacked in their back yard. And they had to put up a battle against a very questionable tire-burning plant that their government officials were trying to lure.

"Please tell me," I wrote to Mr. Harrell, "you are not advocating more Corporate Welfare in the form of tax abatements and other assorted give-aways to those who can already afford to pay their own way." Deals with "town fathers" are ultimately deals with the "taxpayers," only the taxpayers usually don't get a say in the matter.

Carey has low taxes, low electric rates (we own our own distribution system), an updated utilities system, great access to major highways and land to be developed as an industrial park. We are located midway between Columbus and Toledo. Our voters pass school levies. We have four parks and a national shrine located here. We don't need to "cut deals" with anybody.

As a life-long resident and friend of my community, I'd be ashamed and embarrassed to go before town council and ask for hand-outs. Yet perfect strangers will brazenly ask for the world. Shame on them. In nearby towns, fast-food chains and various retailers get aid they don't need while long-time local businesses struggle or fail. I've seen a chain store wheedle tax abatement out of a town and fold up before taxes were finally due.

I hope John is not taking advantage of naive small-town leaders who are giving away the store to entice new business that will eventually ruin the small-town atmosphere that attracted folks in the first place.

I'd like to offer a suggestion to business people who are interested in locating in small towns: The advantages for you are obvious. And, if your business is a good one, the advantages are obvious for the community. But don't show up with your hand out. The rednecks are growing tired of Welfare For the Rich.

Just something for John to think about as he relaxes at his mansion, walks his 50 acres, rides his horses, and putts on his private green out back.

Fixing suburbs and saving small towns

Steve Zender
May 17, 1995

L ast week's issue of Newsweek featured a cover story entitled "Bye-Bye Suburban Dream." Page after page cited the failure of the suburbs. One headline noted that the "new urbanists (whoever they are) want to "take the edge off edge cities. They want to bring small-town charm to blighted metropolitan landscapes."

Ironic, isn't it, how often city people want "small-town charm" and small-town people want to make their towns like the city?

Included in the Newsweek feature was a list entitled "15 ways to fix the suburbs." I didn't know whether to laugh or cry when I read the list. What Newsweek now needs to write is a story called "15 ways to stop small-town people from messing up their towns like the suburbs did."

Will we listen to the people who tell us to appreciate the good things about our rural life? Nah, I doubt it.

Look at number 14 of Newsweek's list, for example: "Turn down the lights." For years, people who sell security lights have been telling farmers they need to light up their places like airport terminals for "safety." When a tiny hamlet like Lovell has "light pollution," as Gene Logsdon has reported, you know we're turning up the lights in dear old Wyandot County, not turning them down.

"Think green." Newsweek lists it as the 15th way to save the suburbs.

" ... pick any spot," says the magazine, "and it's just a matter of time before it makes the magical transition from "countryside" to "real estate." The authors claim the process isn't inevitable. "It's the product of concrete decisions made in an age when roads were still viewed as the harbingers of civilization rather than discount muffler outlets. And as surely as our society made those decisions, it can change them, before lawn meets lawn and asphalt meets asphalt, covering the land in a seamless carpet of sprawl."

But will our society "change the trend?" Will small-town people see their errors in time? Will anyone who has power be able to "think green," as in "grass," rather than as in "money?" Will the ones who see the planning errors be able to win the battle against those who stand to make big money from "development" and don't care if there are planning errors or not?

Listen to the politicians, from the national to the local level, and it's hard to imagine there is any hope for those of us who love little towns. Growth. Jobs. Highways. Money. That's what they talk about and that's how we elect 'em. When politicians like the ones in Ohio put up with dirt and traffic and bad roads and stink and fires and water problems and questionable hiring practices to create low-paying jobs, is there any reason to be optimistic about keeping "small-town charm?"

Newsweek also wants to bring back the corner store, an idea I love, but wonder about. Small-town folks have been deserting their neighborhood stores for years. But maybe there is hope, outside of another oil crisis that makes it too expensive to drive cars out of town.

Other Newsweek ideas: mix housing types; plant trees curbside; hide the garage; make a town center; shrink parking lots. These are ideas which, to a large extent, never left little towns like ours. (Most people probably don't even know it, but Carey has an ordinance which requires landscaping after a parking lot reaches a certain size.)

I especially like Newsweek's number 10: "Plan for mass transit." After my family traversed Washington, D.C., on the Metro system a few years ago, I became a true believer that this was the easy, smart way to move from one place to another. But if any leader in our country ever gets serious about mass transportation, he'd better be a real conservative flag-waver because his patriotism will be questioned.

Mass transportation in America? We've already seen how people react when the government considers cutting a swath through farmland with a highway. Mass transportation will require taking away private property. And mass transportation will be an overt attempt to place less emphasis on the automobile. That's some sort of commie idea, ain't it?

But I'm an optimist, if optimism is hoping all the discount firms in the world go broke and all the Mom and Pop stores make a comeback. Maybe in the not-too-distant future someone will figure out how to make thinking green, as in grass, as profitable as thinking green, as in money.

Taking care of the stories and the pigs

Steve Zender
Aug. 21, 1996

I'll bet it is safe to say that no editor at The Wall Street Journal, The New York Times, The Washington Post, or maybe even the Findlay Courier, has ever received a message like this from a staff writer:

"I'll bring this stuff over Sunday evening or afternoon. It just got too late and the vet was here to take blood samples from the pigs."

In case you're interested, the stories arrived at the office on time and the pigs were okay. Time marches on, but at a slightly different pace out here in the country.

Don't you love it?

Kate, the writer, conducted at least one interview that day, worked in the garden, wrote a couple stories, looked after four kids, and got ready to go on a two-day excursion, all from the comfort of her own home. Well, maybe on a day like that, comfort isn't the right word.

Actually, if I wouldn't be behind the times, I would have never learned about the vet and the pigs. Had I hooked up the modem like I should have done months ago, we would be receiving Kate's stories directly from her computer to ours in the office. As it is, she has to bring us the completed stories on a floppy disk. How backward of us. And I have no excuse for this except that I'm a procrastinator.

My point in reporting this pig story is that out here in rural America, we can have the best of both worlds, or at least part of the best, thanks to technology. Kate can work for a newspaper and do much (not all) of her work from her homestead.

This sort of lifestyle, the "experts" say, will be a growing phenomenon. It's exciting to be part of that.

This past July 10, The Progressor portion of The Progressor-Times celebrated its 28th anniversary. I shudder to think of the equipment we used in those early days – even though our little weekly, believe it or not, was the leader of the pack in technology in those days.

In 1968, the year The Progressor was born, the rest of the newspapers around here were still using the old "hot type" method, setting type in lead on Line-O-Type machines. We were first in the area to use "offset" equipment. But compared to today's computers, it was primitive. The hours were longer and it took more people to do less. And there were no offset printers nearby. We had to drive the paper 80 miles to Wauseon each week to be printed.

Our "innovative" typesetting machine was the Justowriter, an ugly brown typewriter-like contraption which punched out a tape which was then placed in a second ugly brown machine that looked a lot like the first. The second ugly machine clattered along like a high-speed (for those days) typewriter as it spit out the stories. If you made a mistake, too bad, it was already on the tape. The machine had no memory, so if you did it wrong the first time you did it over.

We had a headline machine called the Headliner. You made an adjustment for the size you wanted, turned a big wheel to the letter you desired, and clicked a switch. A light came on to expose the letter on sensitized paper. Photo-mechanical paper, I believe, is what they called it. So you set a headline or an advertisement one letter at a time. Then you ran the exposed paper through chemicals in a little narrow tank. The paper often got stuck in the tank. You saved what you could, cussed quite a bit, and started over.

Next came the Compugraphic era. Compugraphic was a company that catered to little businesses like ours. I can remember they actually put the prices of their equipment in their advertisements. That impressed me. We finally got a memory on some of the machines – one whole line of it – but you still needed chemicals to develop the paper.

We went through a couple of Compugraphic machines, finally progressing to what was called the 7700. Like the other Compugraphics, the big, noisy blue 7700 had film fonts that whirled around in a chamber. When you pressed a letter on the keyboard a light flashed and the proper letter (you hoped) was exposed on the sensitized paper.

That seems like a century ago, even though we've only had our new computer system a few short years.

When the newspaper switched to its present-day computerized system in 1993, I bought three computers, two laser printers, a scanner and the software to run everything. The total cost was less than I had paid for the one Compugraphic 7700 11 years earlier. The capabilities of the computer system over the typesetters aren't even close.

We can now do things of better quality quicker and cleaner and cheaper. And it is more fun. This is progress.

One futurist organization estimates that all the present technological knowledge we now possess will amount to only 1% of what we'll know in 2050. Futurists also claim that improvement in telecommunications will result in people fleeing the cities and moving to rural areas. What does all this mean? I don't know for sure, but I hope it means that people will be able to provide for their families and do important work for their communities while still having time to work in their gardens and take care of the pigs.

Mayberry meets Star Trek

Steve Zender
Dec. 13,1995

George Jones had a recent hit song called "High Tech Redneck." I sit here writing from Carey, Ohio, population 3,600, using the same computer software program used by Time magazine. I think of the song's refrain, part of which says: "I'm a high-tech redneck. Mayberry meets Star Trek."

I've thought a lot about this high-tech redneck idea since the Wall Street Journal's feature about Carey. An amazing amount of information is at our fingertips and it's possible to be as modern and up-to date right here in our little village as anywhere else in the world. (Well, just about.) But most of us out here in the country are content – flattered even – if people see a similarity between our town and that of Sheriff Andy Taylor's.

The Wall Street Journal feature on Carey three weeks ago was a gentle look at small-town life. And it made clear most of us like it here. Clare Ansberry's story – which started on page one and took up a half-page inside – was extremely complimentary, while not making us out as a bunch of saints. It made clear the citizens were proud of what they had and not ashamed to admit they didn't have all the answers.

As communication and ease of travel continue to advance, little places like those in Wyandot County will have a window to the world as large as everyone else. The decision for those who continue to love small towns won't be whether to move into the Star Trek world or not. The challenge will come in trying to preserve Mayberry.

Even though I know The Wall Street Journal is the largest circulated newspaper in the world, I was surprised at the response to Ansberry's story. I expected lots of local response and it was almost universally positive. But I received calls from friends and acquaintances across the country (and I don't have that many friends and acquaintances!) as well as from those I have never met.

A man from Texas called, looking for an artist who was originally from Carey. He told me how envious corporate America is of small-town living. And he was delighted when I had the address and phone number of the artist, who also happened to be a former employee of The Progressor-Times.

A former college friend called from Las Vegas, saying the story made him long for his old home town of Pandora.

A representative of a national magazine in New York inquired about my George Henry manuscript and joked, "I'm ready to move to Carey, Ohio."

The director of marketing at the Plain Dealer in Cleveland wrote a letter, saying the story confirmed his suspicion ". . . that love is alive in small town America."

A man in California said the story brought tears to his eyes and sent $10 to put flowers on the grave of George Henry Bish.

A fellow from Tiffin phoned to praise the village and urge me to "never let the people of your community forget that story." He said people need to be reminded of how fortunate they are.

His point is well taken. We do take too much for granted. We get caught up in the glitzy, glamourized hype of movies and television, longing for things we probably really don't want and forgetting how wonderful it is to live out here in the country, imperfect as it may be, but among family and friends.

It was like going to church

Gene Logsdon
Sept. 7, 1994

The latest government celebration to honor the God of Cannibalistic Pseudo-Capitalism in Upper Sandusky reminded me of going to church. About a hundred of the Republican Faithful stood around in the bright August sunshine, occasionally looking skyward as if expecting the Holy Spirit to descend and bless them with the gift of tongues. Instead Bishop Voinovich came down by state police helicopter, not a bad way to add to the Pentecostal aura of the occasion.

Flanked by Archbishop Oxley and lesser prelates Randy Weston and Karen Gillmor (they had come by car), the Bishop moved smoothly through the sacramental rubrics of groundbreaking and ribbon-cutting, and then took to the pulpit, as did the Archbishop, to proclaim the glories of economic growth, especially when financed by the tax money dispensed by Republicans buying votes. Archbishop Oxley did not disappoint his flock, finding a way to belittle the Washington Post, that stupid rag of the stupid liberals, even though the Post had published an article complimentary to Bishop Voinovich.

The big things in life are the little things

After the holy water of tax money had been sprinkled upon Mayor Richardson ($150,000) and multinational mega-company, Guardian Industries ($30,000), we enjoyed a communion repast of tasty food and drink in the new spec building recently purchased by Cobra Industries. Good will blossomed among us and we lingered, as we do on the church steps after services, to chat and joke with people whom we know we are going to be angry at again by the middle of the week. Even Archbishop Oxley spoke amicably to me although I doubt he knew he was talking to his chief critic – perhaps only critic – in the Republican Black Forest region of northwestern Ohio. And even I think he is a much better politician than anything the poor Democrats can muster against him.

"Isn't this wonderful?" he asked, shaking my hand.

"Oh, I don't know," I answered. "I can't think of a worse way to live than traveling around constantly gladhanding people like you have to do."

"I love it," he said. "It's very invigorating to me to assist in all this progress. We just came from a similar groundbreaking in Bucyrus and are on our way to another one."

"But that's just the problem to me," I replied. "Every town around is doing exactly the same thing Upper Sandusky is doing. We end up no better off in our competitive relationship with each other than we were before, except we've spent a lot of taxpayer money."

He looked at me incredulously again and said, "Well, I'd rather do this than go to funerals."

I don't know if he meant that figuratively or literally, but either way I suppose it was a pretty good answer. Nevertheless, I am surprised that very few of the Faithful agree with what I'm trying to say. Is it smart to do the same things that Bucyrus, Marion, Tiffin, Findlay, Lima, etc., etc., are doing in the way of extra sewer, water, roads, spec building and tax breaks? All that the towns are doing is setting themselves up to be taken advantage of by business. Every town will soon have spec buildings running out of their ears. So who will sell or rent theirs the cheapest? Who will give the biggest tax break? Who is most adept at paving the way to the Bishop for more business welfare money? We are setting up a system that will have more potential for graft than outright socialism.

The final result of all this is a huge welfare program for corporate America under the notion that government knows how to "invest" money better than individual citizens to create more jobs. I plan to vote for Bishop

Voinovich again, but his unquestioning faith in jobs as an excuse to funnel tax money to business is pseudo-capitalistic religion (actually it is socialism), not necessarily economic fact. First of all, the practice too easily becomes just a hypocritical way to buy votes. Secondly, have you seen the statistics? There are more jobs being created now, yes, but they are mostly part-time jobs (so industry can avoid paying benefits) or they are lower paying jobs.

More jobs is no more the automatic result of paying welfare to business than they are the automatic result of paying welfare to poor people. Saying otherwise is just another way to "speak in tongues."

That's Governor Voinovich with the shovel, Mayor Richardson, at left, and Mike Oxley next to him.

Lots of suits. None of them Santa's

Steve Zender
Oct. 13, 1993

There were more suits in Carey last Thursday than you see at most weddings.

The town was dressed up to see the state's director of development. Donald Jakeway started his Wyandot County visit in Carey at 7:30 a.m. (Actually, he was a little late and the suits had to wait. He was coming from Findlay and got behind school buses on 568.) Business and government officials seemed happy to meet him.

I was pleased to hear many of his comments and delighted to see Jakeway wasn't dressed in a red suit, dispensing Christmas presents. Years ago when Governor James Rhodes boarded a campaign bus after making all sorts of lavish promises, a local fellow leaned over to me and asked, "Was that the governor or Santa Claus?"

No, Jakeway didn't come across as Santa. He wasn't making big promises of big gifts. He wasn't even telling us, exactly, what was naughty and nice. How did he foresee small towns in the future? He essentially said that small towns would have to decide that for themselves. Granted, it wasn't a direct answer, but I liked it anyway.

Sure, there were plenty of people who could have informed the director that this newspaper has writers who cast a cynical eye on state and local bureaucrats making plans the general public doesn't like. But let's try to put our skepticism aside.

Jakeway said any plan must take into account a wide variety of ideas, opinions and hopes for the future. It's such a simple, common-sense idea. But it is so often forgotten when people in suits get together in an enclosed room.

"Is this all really worth anything?" I was quietly asked after the lunch at Woody's last week. Jakeway had given a brief, upbeat talk; he had turned over a check to the City of Upper Sandusky, and presented a $33,322 Ohio Industrial Training Program grant to representatives from Continental Hose (well, maybe there was the hint of Christmas in the air). Jakeway had been presented a basket by the Upper and Carey Chambers of Commerce, filled with products made in Wyandot County. There had been good food at Woody's and even a few laughs. But, as my questioner wondered, was this worth anything?

I had no doubt that it was worth **something.** But the question was what? And was the something good or bad?

As I looked around at us all, I had the sense that this group of men and women could accomplish a lot of "good." But that wasn't a sure thing. The people who met Director Jakeway represented a tiny fraction of Wyandot County. By incorrectly thinking their opinions reflect the public's opinion, this group of people could also lead the county down the wrong path.

Although he didn't say so directly, Jakeway's comments in Carey indicate he understands this. He stressed teamwork, but more than once he mentioned diversity of opinion. He cautioned against making plans without first knowing what your community wants.

I'd like to think that since Jakeway is originally from a small town himself, he is more in tune with what small-town citizens consider "good." Here are a few things I think community developers should remember.

• The results of any survey I've ever seen has said people like living in Carey or Sycamore or Upper Sandusky because they like what is commonly known as the "small-town atmosphere." They like the quiet and the safety. They cherish the friendships they develop in a little town. This is something anyone doing any kind of developing should have first and foremost in their mind. Most citizens in a small town want to **keep** their town small.

• The above point does not mean that all forms of development will be opposed by residents. Most surveys will also show that many people express a desire for more jobs and services. This means they want **some** growth.

• Community leaders should remember that when the locals say they want more business and industry, they aren't asking for communities to turn into prostitutes. When the government, whether it is local, state or federal, is selling itself in the form of tax abatements or some other form of monetary inducement, the typical citizen is bright enough to know the government is playing the game with their hard-earned tax dollars. The average citizen wants new business to come to their community if that business is going to be a positive influence. And the business should be lured to a town because of what the community has to offer in the way of location, or low electric rates, or a good labor force, not because what we're willing to give away.

• Most people in small towns aren't much interested in "increasing their property values." They'll keep their place in a state of good repair, thank you, but when you're not planning on selling, the only thing high property values get you is higher taxes. By the same token, most people aren't going to be happy if their government hurts their property value by inviting in some pollution belching firm that provides more headaches than it cures.

• Small-town residents are usually concerned about their schools. And, more likely than not, they want to keep them small. Any community developer should ask school officials if they'd like to see a lot of growth. More likely than not, the answer will be no.

• Lovers of small towns, if they've thought about it much, realize that "development" is a double-edged sword. Government officials brag about the tax money (**your** tax money) they have funnelled into one project or another. What's never mentioned by these people are the businesses that get hurt by such projects. For every grant that is given to a restaurant, a retail store or an industry, there will be a business in the same field who is now operating under a handicap imposed by a government hand-out to someone else.

So why try to "develop" anything in a small town? Maybe to make a good thing even better. Even the folks in Mayberry occasionally envied the amenities over in Mt. Pilot! But little towns should proceed with caution. Wyandot County communities don't need to get caught up in the freebie frenzy that often results in an overrun infrastructure which eventually winds up in higher taxes for a public that didn't want all this commotion in the first place.

Small communities should be prepared to inform and assist prospective businesses and new residents. Guidelines should be set up for the present and the future. But at every stage of a community's growth, leaders should be asking, "Who will benefit from this?"

And always remember, no matter what kind of suit he's wearing, that's not Santa Claus working for the government.

Tall tales of Wyandot County

Gene Logsdon
June 21, 1978

M any stories float around about the late Ward Walton, one of our most illustrious citizens. I admired him greatly. When I was laying tile on one of his farms south of Columbus, the hearsay talk said he was the biggest landowner east of the Mississippi. I was afraid to ask him if that were true. Or if the story told to illustrate that claim were true. I preferred just to believe it all, true or not.

According to the story, Ward was driving through the countryside in southern Ohio looking for cheap land to buy, as was his favorite pastime. He happened by a rundown farm, buildings abandoned, fence sagging, weeds growing up in field corners. Just the kind of farm he could sometimes buy right. Hurrying into the county seat, he looked up the farm to see who the owner might be. Turned out to be Ward Walton.

And everybody likes to retell the one about how Ward and his brother Howard gave each other hell for not getting one field of corn picked. Each thought it belonged to the other.

Tall tales of Wyandot County

My favorite story of Wyandot County is about Walter Vogel, who was not a farmer but owner of a shoe store, the same his son now operates. Walter had parked his brand new car in front of the store. When he went to back out, the car was not in reverse, but in drive, which startled him as it would anyone. But, unused to automatic transmissions and not all that accustomed to any collection of pistons, Walter jammed down with his right foot, under which he was accustomed to finding a brake. His foot, however, was still on the gas pedal. The new car bolted friskily forward, careening smack dab into his plate glass window, while Walter hauled back on the steering wheel for all he was worth, shouting, "Whoa, dammit, whoa!"

Now it's Fred McCarthy who is immortalizing himself in county history. His recent adventure will no doubt be enlarged and enhanced as time goes by, especially since his sons Charlie and Ed are two of the best storytellers in this neck of the woods. (Ed says he went out to drive a tractor for Charlie one night, the tractor according to Charlie to be sitting in such and such a field by such and such a road. Ed plowed all night, only to find by dawn's early light that he had turned over 40 acres for Leonard Rall.) Fred is well past retirement age, but he drives for Charlie when he can and some of the other tractor drivers say that Fred can still lay out a straighter furrow than any of them.

So here was Fred, whose hands have made shiny the handles of horse plows, tooling along in the night, working ground from the glass-enclosed cab of a humongous four-wheel-drive beast, each tire of which was big enough to hold a team of horses. As he turned at the end of the field about midnight, he might have noticed a slight tug on the drawbar, a momentary gasp of the monstrous motor. But then again he might not have. Halfway across the endless landscape of clods, he became aware that the night was even blacker than usual. The flickering lights of farmhouses on the horizon had disappeared. Hmmmmm. Fred looked out back of the cab. The lights of the tractor picked out something following him stealthily across the field. By God, it was an electric utility pole.

And that ain't all. Attached to the pole was a half mile of Ohio Power's finest electric line. It was hours before power was restored to the area.

Used to be every thunderstorm brought a power failure. Now every time Ma sees a 40-foot field cultivator go by with its wings folded up like a hungry vulture, she fills the bathtub with water and gets the kerosene lamp out.

What would the Eden board have thought?

Steve Zender
Oct. 3, 1991

I just received the latest standardized test scores from the State of Ohio. It will take some time to digest all the information, but I couldn't help but wonder what the Eden Township Board of Education would have thought about all that information back in 1930.

Miss Myrtle Crumrine (Mrs. Sanders to the students in my seventh grade class at Carey and Mrs. Dible to those who know her today) began her teaching career in 1930 and I would suspect there were few who could imagine that anyone would be receiving anything like the computerized package of information that arrived at the newspaper office Monday.

Miss Crumrine, just a youngster herself in 1930, was probably too busy building the fire and oiling the floors in the Melmore school to concern herself with computerized test scores, even if there would have been such a thing.

Read her contract and you'll probably come to one of two conclusions: Teachers were overworked and underpaid in 1930; or they are underworked and overpaid in 1991. Maybe it is really a combination of the two.

That, I suppose, could be said for just about any profession. (Journalism excluded, of course.)

Mrs. Crumrine's pay, as specified in that contract signed 61 years ago, was set at $800 for a term of 34 weeks. She did, at least, receive $10 for janitor's fees. The $800 was doled out in nine monthly installments. The teacher had to wait until the final payment of the year to collect for her janitorial work. The Eden school board must have been a tough bunch!

According to the contract, the teacher was expected to build a fire "not later than 8 o'clock a.m. in cold weather." Opening of school doors could be postponed until 8:30 a.m. in warm weather.

In addition to being required to stay on the school premises from the time of opening and during recess and noon, the teacher was expected to supervise games on the playgrounds and to control the kids at all times.

Teacher Bob Hayman and an Eden class in the early 1950s.

There were specific instructions such as "prevent abuse of the smaller pupils by the larger ones." Another requirement was to "thoroughly prepare and study in advance the subject matter to be taught each day so that same will be presented most efficiently to pupils." And there was this harbinger of computerized printouts: the teacher was supposed to "File monthly report with county superintendent, and copy of the report with the clerk of Board of

Education." Presto! Sixty-one years later and you have reams of reports that hardly anyone can decipher.

As if building the fire and teaching the kids weren't enough, Miss Crumrine was expected to keep the room "free from floating dust particles by applying floor oil to floor whenever it is necessary." (Hey, the woman was getting $10 a year for this!) The Eden board did have the decency to note, right in the contract, the following: "Oil to be furnished by Board of Education."

Maybe times were simpler then, but there has always been some form of bureaucracy. In 1930 the teacher was expected to "follow course of study and instructions as outlined by county superintendent; district superintendent; music supervisor; and the board of education.

And then there was the final paragraph of the contract: "The Board of Education favors the plan of opening the morning session of the school by the teacher reading a select passage of Scripture from the Holy Bible, not to teach sectarianism, but because the Bible contains the noblest gems of thought and the purest code of morals the world has ever known."

This rule would obviously run into trouble with the law today, but what do you expect in a place called Eden?

Stay in your own yard

Steve Zender
Jan. 3, 1990

My mother's mother was born a Baptist; my Dad's family was Catholic, and I was eventually raised a Lutheran. I figure I had a first-hand look at the ecumenical movement long before it was popularized.

I like to believe being raised this way gave me a healthy respect for another person's religious point of view, so it bothers me when I've occasionally been accused of picking on religion. The accusation usually comes from someone who (in my opinion) has an inflated opinion of their self worth and would like to impose their own beliefs on everyone else.

My idea of religious freedom is to think of it in its truest sense, and that includes the right to be non-religious if you want to be. I enjoy – I admit it – poking fun at hypocritical acts and words done in the name of religion. And it happens so often it could supply me with material for a lifetime of columns.

The big things in life are the little things

One thing I have been unable to understand is why so-called religious people hurt each other so often under the guise of doing something in the name of God. When Moslems put out death contracts on writers; or Protestants and Catholics shoot each other in Northern Ireland; or televangelists bilk their flock out of millions of dollars; or local ministers attempt to get people arrested, as they did at the Carey festival, I am always bewildered. Being upset by these random acts of hatred is not being against religion, it is being against hypocrisy. Unfortunately the craziness is not confined to any one religion.

After years of defending Catholics, I was dismayed, as a kid, to have my boss, who was Catholic, make fun of a small church that was being opened in town. "They've got as much right to their beliefs as you do to yours," I argued. My boss grudgingly conceded that point, I guess, but he told me something I've never forgotten: "My religion is the toughest to live with, but it's the best to die with." Had that been said to me today, I would have told him I wasn't sure about the dead part, but being allowed to smoke, drink, dance and gamble didn't seem too tough of rules to me. I find many religions tougher to live with. "Toughness," to my way of thinking, doesn't make one religion better than another.

But if you try to be truly open-minded, you won't be able to defend one side too long. You no sooner fight for the rights of those little store-front churches across the land and you find they've grown into Jerry, Jimmy and Tammy Faye and they're trying to force their beliefs down the throats of everybody else. They're telling the schools what to teach, the newspapers what to print, the television what to air and the people who to vote for. You can't help but feel a little frustrated if you're in the news business because you know that the same people who are griping about the liberal media are using it to advance their own social agenda.

My dad tells about the time the Ku Klux Klan burned a cross in the yard of his parents. My grandmother, who had to stand on her tiptoes to get to five feet tall, marched out on the lawn, waded into the crowd, and began calling some of the hooded people by name. She told them to get the hell out of her yard. And they did.

I suppose my grandmother summed up my philosophy on religious freedom that day: Believe what you want. Just stay in your own yard.

Don't listen to the "best times of your life " speech

Steve Zender
June 1, 1994

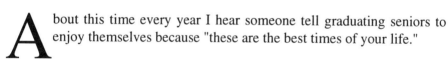

About this time every year I hear someone tell graduating seniors to enjoy themselves because "these are the best times of your life."

This never fails to depress me.

If the best times are over at 18, the most popular graduation gift should be a visit from Jack Kevorkian.

"These are the best times of your life." What a bleak message to give to a young person. Why not just say: "You've had your fun. It's all downhill from here. Get ready for a lifetime of headaches, disappointment and misery."

I like to think the best is yet to come, no matter what your age. For our graduates, I hope there is an enjoyable job out there; a good family; exciting places to see; new people to meet; new challenges; mysteries to solve; wonders to behold; something to learn. Sure, a person's life might seem to be in reverse from time to time throughout the years – or at least in neutral – but young people should never believe their best days are over

The big things in life are the little things

when, in actuality, students are just beginning on what should be an exciting journey.

I assume these "best days of your life" people are referring to the fact that kids don't have money problems or families to support or as many decisions to make. They don't have "responsibilities." But anyone who thinks young people don't have problems or worries has forgotten what it was like to be a kid. Teenage years can be troubling, confusing times. And even the well-adjusted teenagers, if they are active in school, certainly take on their share of responsibilities.

While high school days are important and provide cherished memories, if the high points of a life are the days as a student or an athlete or a musician in high school, then the rest of the time on the planet has been a dismal failure.

Humans should keep trying to compile "best times of our life" moments all through life.

I have a class reunion coming up this month. I remember the Class of 1964 as being bright, mischievous and confident. We'll reminisce and I'm sure most of us will believe we had an even greater time in high school than we really did. The ones who had a really miserable time probably won't be at the class reunion because they don't want to relive terrible moments. During all this remembering, someone is sure to say those high school days were the "best times of our lives." And I'll hope that person really doesn't mean that. It's sad to think you would have left your best days lie in a classroom 30 years ago.

Please do something, governor

Steve Zender
April 17, 1974

D ear Governor Gilligan:

There is a crime being committed daily near Carey, Ohio, that I think you should know about. Apparently the Ohio Department of Transportation doesn't really give a damn. We get promises and reassurances that the criminal activity will be stopped, but no action from the state.

People older, and supposedly wiser, than myself say, "Be patient. The problem will be corrected." Well, governor, I recently watched the fifth person die at the 23-15 intersection near my home town. I have had it with "being patient." I don't like to watch people die. I don't think you would either and I think it is about time you used the power of your office to get the people in the department of transportation off their behinds before another person gets run over and killed or hurt.

The big things in life are the little things

The last accident at our infamous intersection occurred on Good Friday. That Good Friday left two little boys without a mother or a father. The memories of two little faces, trapped in a wrecked car, bleeding, crying, while a mother's life drains away isn't recorded in the statistics kept by the department of transportation.

If a sniper had been sitting at the same intersection since 1968 and had picked off five travelers and wounded nearly 100 more and caused an unrecorded amount of property damage month after month, Carey would have National Guard units patrolling its streets. Since the killing and the maiming is being done by automobiles, the situation goes unnoticed by the governor.

It doesn't go unnoticed by those of us who live here. It doesn't go unnoticed by families of those who have died on U.S. 23.

I read the safety news releases issued by your safety director. They're sickeningly funny. If the state wants safety, install an interchange at the 23-15 intersection.

I read of the state's safety slogan contest. That saddens me too. I see the governor's "Number one" license plate goes to the contest winner. How about offering another award, an award for those who have died and those who have been injured at this intersection. The prize would be your cutting red tape and getting an interchange built at the intersection near Carey. It would be a lasting memorial to those who have been killed by the state's engineering folly that, unfortunately, is located near my home town.

Maybe after reading this letter, you'll decide to pass on the 23-15 interchange idea for research. If that's what you have in mind, don't bother. I've seen those agencies at work. I've had my telephone calls transferred from Columbus to Bowling Green to Lima while subordinates, assistants, spokesmen and flunkies try to decide exactly who has responsibility for this mess. I've seen the transportation department change the intersection lights from stop lights to caution signals. And I've seen three people killed and accident after accident since that change was made.

Apparently no one in this little town of 3,500 has the power to get things done promptly when it comes to dealing with the DOT. I think you do have that authority. The people of this village have been waiting for years to see the 23-15 grade crossing done away with and an interchange built. If my hunch is correct, they are going to wait more years unless somebody says "Correct the problem. Correct it now."

Please do something, governor

Maybe I'm being too idealistic in requesting that something be done immediately. If I am, I'm sorry. Not sorry for asking but sorry that you can't do anything about the situation.

I hope you can help. I'm anxiously awaiting your reply. So are the rest of the residents in Carey, Ohio.

We have been patient for long enough. No, we have been too patient for too long.

Editor's note: The governor's office responded to this column several days after it was written. On May 20, 1974, just over a month after the column was published, Governor John Gilligan made a trip to Carey to announce that an interchange project, then valued at $867,000, was under way at Carey's U.S. 23-Ohio 15 intersection.

The people around us

"What would I ever do with the money?

Gene Logsdon
From Dec. 31, 1980

A t the age of 100, Gottlieb Seiler still killed groundhogs with his cane.

I had the privilege of meeting Mr. Seiler back in 1963, nine years before he died at 102. I doubt that he would appreciate being remembered for killing a groundhog, because he was a tenderer man than that anecdote implies, and killed groundhogs for the same reason I or any other country people kill them: Now that man has destroyed the balance of nature in regard to rodents, someone better kill some of them or they will undermine (literally) human civilization, at least in Ohio. Gottlieb Seiler was one of the most deeply committed environmentalists I know. In the same way, Gottlieb Seiler did not attend church very often, but he was a deeply spiritual man. To my thinking, he possessed wisdom, a word little used anymore.

Wisdom is not fashionable. Half the world bows to scientific intellectualism and the other half to religious emotionalism. The former wants us to embrace the computer, the latter wants us to embrace the person in the next pew. It is no wonder that wisdom hides in a groundhog hole.

"My grandfather was one of a kind," says Homer Seiler. "I don't think he trusted progress. I think it looked dangerous to him and maybe he was right. When the new highway (U.S. 23) went by his house, he was appalled at the flow of traffic. He'd often say, 'Where are all these people going?' And I never could think of a good answer to that question. That was the effect he'd have on us. He'd make us think."

"He was one of the sharpest men I've known," says Ronnie Huffman, who farmed Seiler's place awhile and finally bought it. "He believed in a lot of old sayings that sounded a little superstitious, only I learned that nine times out of 10, they came true.

"He loved the land. He farmed his 56 acres with a team of horses. Kept a few cows and a few sows. And he did all right in his day. He had money when he died. But he was content with his life. He didn't try to squeeze every cent possible from the land.

"When I farmed for him on the half and he got too old to take care of his cows, he insisted that we maintain a four-year rotation with clover hay to keep the soil fertility up. He knew that if you row-crop this kind of ground continuously you'd eventually end up with nothing. You have to take care of your land just like you have to take care of your health."

Seiler obviously took care of his health to live vigorously to age 100. Dr. Schoolfield in Upper Sandusky recalls him fondly. "I knew him professionally for many years, but we were also good friends," says Dr. Schoolfield. "He impressed me with his mental attitude. Very alert. Always curious about life and the world. But I think he lived so long in reasonably good health because he didn't worry about whether he was going to live or die. He never worried about anything so far as I noticed."

"I only remember him really getting upset once," says Huffman. "When the state came through buying land for the new highway. He believed the power of eminent domain was a terrible injustice. Finally he was even able to accept that philosophically. He said he'd never live to see the road completed anyway. But he did. Someone asked him once why he didn't put running water in his house. He said it was too much of a bother. And that he'd be dead before he'd get any use out of it anyway. But he went right on living, using the windmill and pumpjack outside. He didn't even have a television set until the last couple of years, when he was given one."

What would I ever do with the money?

"I remember clearly what he said when I asked him once if he were interested in selling his farm," recalls Dennis Barnes, Upper Sandusky realtor. "He replied: 'What would I ever do with the money?' That was the first, but not the last time I've heard that remark in similar circumstances. Makes a person sit down and think about just what is the true meaning of success."

Huffman nods and smiles at that recollection. "Gottlieb had a favorite expression about money you didn't really need. He'd say, 'Well, you can always stick it in your eye, I guess.' I asked him regularly if I could buy his farm, but he'd always say there was 'no way I'd sell it.' But he watched the way I farmed for him and the years went by and one day he just up and said: 'You've ding-donged me to buy this place for 12 years. You still interested?' I said I was and he said, 'I'm getting to the point where I want to know who this land goes to. Will you let me go on living here?' And so we wrote it right into the contract that he could go on living there until he died, and that's the way it worked out."

Old Gottlieb Seiler knew what he was doing. He wanted to make sure his farm did not die with him – that it would go to someone who would take care of it properly. Huffman not only continues the clover rotations on the farm, he does one better. He lets one alfalfa cutting (of three) lay on the ground, mowed but unmade, to rot back into the ground for humus. This is a practice almost unheard of among today's debt-frantic farmers. It demands a sacrifice of a little short-term income. "Actually, the practice pays in the long run," says Huffman. "Oh, it looks like you are losing a little money here and now, but that kind of money is" – he gropes for the right words, then smiles – "well, you can always stick it in your eye."

Aunt
Leopa
1908-1996

Steve Zender
From Aug. 28, 1996

I wonder if I'll ever know another person so willing to live but so prepared to die.

My Aunt Leopa died last Friday. She was 88. What wonderful memories I have of Aunt Leopa and Uncle Toay. (I was nearly a teenager before I realized it was Uncle Toay – a nickname given to him as a kid because he was a towhead – and not Uncle Toy.) He died years ago, so my children did not have the pleasure of knowing him. But they knew Aunt Leopa (Aunt Opie to them), and they, like everyone else who knew her, loved her.

Especially vivid are my memories of the times my cousin Tom and I spent at Aunt Leopa and Uncle Toay's humble cottage in Indiana. No TV or indoor plumbing for a week. As kids, we visited each and every summer.

In the early days we fished with cane poles. Later we advanced to the rod and reel. We cleaned our own fish, got to drink coffee, and we behaved ourselves, else we'd get "backhanded" by Uncle Toay. At least that's what he always threatened.

Aunt Leopa

We knew we weren't allowed to swim right after we ate, and that Aunt Leopa expected to know where we were every minute of the day.

We rowed their skinny little wooden boat out on the lake (never by ourselves, mind you) to fish for blue gill or rock bass. It wasn't until much later they powered the old gray craft with a tiny gasoline engine.

There were very few kids around, but sometimes we played "flies and grounders" with a couple of Uncle Toay's nephews who summered in a cottage across the way.

As far as I can recall, neither Tom nor I ever got "backhanded," but then we never pushed our luck much. Some people just have that knack of being able to command respect without force.

Aunt Leopa was a deeply religious woman. I can't even begin to know all the people she took in, looked after, cared for, gave money to, and prayed for.

Like most other Zenders, she had that temper that flared up quickly and subsided just as fast. She didn't much like to lose at euchre and it would be best not to argue religion or politics with her. She wasn't perfect, but if she's not in heaven, the place is empty.

There were 16 kids in my dad's family and since last August, three of them have died. First was Uncle Paul. (He once played Santa Claus but after he left I told my parents that wasn't Santa, that was Uncle Paul.) Then it was ornery Uncle Dick. When he was still a chain-smoker, I asked him how he could possibly smoke more than four packs of cigarettes a day. "You've got to get up early and stay up late," he said.

And now Aunt Leopa. Wherever she was, there was laughter nearby.

Last week Tom and I talked to an old fellow we knew from those weeks at the lake. When I was a kid, I knew Andrew reminded me of someone famous, but I couldn't quite figure out who. As we shook hands when he arrived at the funeral home that day I suddenly realized it was Henry Fonda.

As Andrew prepared to leave, we shook hands again. "Well, I'll probably never see you two again," he said to Tom and me. He paused and pointed his finger to the sky. "Unless it's up there." Our cousin Donald, Aunt Leopa's son, was standing there and he stepped back and asked incredulously, "These two guys?"

Aunt Leopa would have liked that one.

Renewing your faith in humanity

Gene Logsdon
Oct. 5, 1994

With all the bad news and lies and corruption that pour out of Washington, it is nice to be able to relate a true story that will renew your faith in humanity. And in this instance, it took some home folks to make it happen.

Don and Joey Dannenhauer, who for many years have owned an insurance business and a laundromat in Nevada, have a son, Michael, who is President Bush's travel scheduler, now and when Mr. Bush was in office. How's that for a "local boy makes good?" But that's not the story I want to tell just now, although the story directly involves Michael.

Once when Mr. Bush was still in office, Don and Joey went to Washington to visit Michael. Michael in turn had arranged for them to meet the president, which was fairly easy for him to do because his office was right off the Oval Office.

Don and Joey had the unique pleasure of chatting with the president of the United States. "The president was just as friendly and considerate to us as if we were old friends and he had all the time in the world," says Don,

The Dannenhauers, from left: Michael, Natalie Jo and D.C., with President Bush.

"even though there were a couple of generals outside waiting impatiently to discuss the latest crisis in Kuwait."

The telephone rang. The president was in conversation with the Dannenhauers, so Michael answered the phone, as he sometimes does. He listened intently. The president and the Dannenhauers stopped talking to stare at Michael. Michael, on the phone, grinned, rolled his eyes, and then said: "It's for you, Dad. David has a problem with the washers in the laundromat."

President Bush magnanimously nodded Don to the phone. If the laundromats of the nation weren't working, the country was in deep trouble. First things first. So while the most powerful man in the world waited, and his generals outside the door waited, Don instructed David on what he had to do to get things operating properly back in Nevada, Ohio.

Now **that's** America!

Gertrude Stubbs was a pioneer in women's sports

Gene Logsdon
March 29, 1996

Gertrude Stubbs was named Citizen of the Year in Upper Sandusky for a lot better reasons than her background in sports, but it is kind of nice that she should receive the honor in the year the Lady Rams played their best basketball ever.

I think it comes as a surprise to most people that high schools encouraged women's sports way back in the 1920s. Mrs. Stubbs, whom many of us think of as Fairhaven Retirement Home's "Angel of Mercy," played varsity basketball all of her four years at Norwalk from 1925 to 1929. After high school she played what was called "independent" basketball (what we'd call semi-pro) for four more years. "The players were mostly from our high school team," she says. "The owner of Keller's Newsstand in Norwalk sponsored us, and the local dentist was our manager. We were called the Keller Newsies. We didn't get paid, except for food and travel cost, but we played all over Ohio and won most of our games, as we had in high school."

They even played a men's team once. "The boys thought they were going to have an easy time of it," Mrs. Stubbs remembers, "but they had to keep their first team on the floor and then only won by a few points."

In high school in the 1920s, girls played basketball in pleated skirts and blouses. "If I remember correctly, the blouses were called knitty blouses," she says. "When we played independent ball, we got to wear shorts like the boys."

For fear that it would sound like boasting, she made me promise not to repeat the congratulatory newspaper headline with her name in bold type that appeared after one of the team's victories. (I didn't promise not to talk **about** the headline. If you check out the Norwalk paper from

The Keller Newsies. That's Gertrude Stubbs in the top row at left.

1930-33, I bet you can find that headline. Her maiden name was Ballwig.) "You can imagine how well that went over at home," she says, laughing. "We played three nights a week, but I was trying to keep my mother from finding that out."

She was not only good in basketball, but tennis too. "I was the tennis champion in high school. I love that game, too." She says it as if, at 85, she is toying with the idea of getting her racket out again this spring.

The big things in life are the little things

As a Keller Newsie, she was also working full time at a law office in Norwalk. What with roads and cars of the early 1930s, I can imagine that she stayed almost as fully occupied then as she does today with a full schedule of volunteer work in the community. In 1933 she met Don Stubbs (now deceased) and they married in 1934. "The team disbanded after the 1933 season," she says. "I don't know if we were unusual. Just a group of girls who loved playing basketball so much that after high school we stayed together and kept on playing until marriage and careers came our way. I don't think any of us were quite good enough to become pros, even if we had that choice. But we sure had fun."

Shortly after those years, women's sports declined drastically. "I don't really know why," says Mrs. Stubbs. Sports historians say that in the Roaring Twenties, women dared to do things unheard of before, but by the time the sobering decade of the Thirties set in, more conservative attitudes prevailed. "My father-in-law teased me so much about my basketball days that I burned up most of the memorabilia and news clipping I had collected," says Mrs. Stubbs, laughing again.

Her father-in-law was, of course, Charles Stubbs, who ran Commercial Bank for about a thousand years, it seems to me. He gave me a lollipop every month when I deposited my 30 shiny new pennies, each of which Grandfather Rall gave me for opening the driveway gate for him every morning when he came out to the farm. Lollipops were hard to come by then.

Gertrude says she was "totally flabbergasted" by her Citizen of the Year award. She looks forward to the banquet honoring her on April 25 for a number of reasons, not the least of which is that her great-granddaughter, age four, will be there too.

There's a little restaurant in Monroeville, just west of Norwalk, owned by the son of one of the Keller Newsie players, where you will see a picture of that long-ago pioneer team on the wall. In 1930, the Keller Newsies were, due to the times, even more sensational than the Lady Rams are today. You young players, basking in your well-earned glory, might want to give a tip of the hat to Gertrude when you see her and thank her for pioneering the idea, now taken for granted, that women ought to have a chance to live fuller lives just like men.

It's a girl – again

Steve Zender
Oct. 7, 1981

M y prediction came true. It was another girl. The doctors would say no more than "It'll be a baby." But I knew it would be a girl, despite all the prognostications of a boy from friends, neighbors and relatives.

How did I know? Well, my reasoning is unscientific, to be sure, but I figured that after being an only child, therefore having no sibling rivalry to contend with throughout my childhood, fate would see to it that I would grow to be an old man by getting constantly outvoted by four women (wife included).

I'm not complaining. Girls are fine with me. The biggest problem fathers of three girls have is convincing others that we weren't crushed because that third kid wasn't a boy.

Fathers of girls, when they tell folks, "I really don't care what we have," are used to getting that look from people which silently says, "Now I know better than that."

The big things in life are the little things

But it is true, at least with some of us, that baby girls are just fine. As a matter of fact, when Sarah, our second daughter, was born, the doctor forgot to tell us immediately what we had – and my wife and I never thought to ask. The doctor finally said something like, "By the way, you have a girl."

As I see it, the biggest problem with girls, as opposed to boys, is that I must spend the next several years convincing the girls that big weddings really are a waste of money.

Sue likes to tell people that energetic Sarah is actually twin boys disguised in a little girl's body. Following in the footsteps of Amy and Sarah, Molly runs a great risk. Either this kid is going to be boring by comparison or the two older ones will give her so many bad ideas that Mom and Dad may need therapy in the near future.

Right now, the greatest difficulty is convincing the two other children that baby need not be awake constantly. Nor does baby need to be held for 24 hours each day. When not holding the baby we've found that sisters of newborns feel they must either:

1. Run.
2. Wrestle.
3. Yell.
4. Jump.
5. Cheer.

At times they do one through five simultaneously.

As a matter of fact, that's what little girls do even when they don't have baby sisters. I've already discovered that parents of girls are able to speak to four-year-olds only while the kids are doing all of the above or:

6. Standing on their head.

When they grow a little older, say about nine or so, the girls do all of the above but add the snapping of fingers, clapping of hands, singing (sort of) and talking on the telephone.

More experienced parents tell me the talking on the telephone part intensifies with age. There are predictions from some parents that we should consider purchasing an individual phone line for the kids. My first reaction is to say, "We'll have none of that separate line stuff in this house!" but I've eaten too many words in less than 10 years to ever utter such a statement.

It's too early to worry about phones. I'm just trying to get in good enough physical shape to talk to three daughters as they run and jump through life.

He liked people

Steve Zender
Dec. 29.1983

It was fitting that another of his grandchildren was born on Dec. 20, the day he died. Anyone who knew Russ Mewhorter, knew how much he loved his grandkids.

Little Jennifer Sue, born to the youngest of the Mewhorter children, is doing fine. Her biggest misfortune is that she will never meet her grandfather personally. But she will hear about him. Memories of this very special man will live on.

Life, as the cliche goes, sometimes seems unfair, but I doubt if my father-in-law spent much time worrying about that. I know he suffered terrible pain when he lost his 20-year-old son, Doug, in an automobile accident. But I never heard him ask, why my son? He suffered through polio as a child and a severe breathing problem as an adult. But you can ask his children and they'll tell you they can't remember him complaining about either.

The only indication he gave that his breathing problem had worsened was when he readily agreed to a serious operation, one from which he never recovered.

The big things in life are the little things

I'm sure he wondered about the fairness of life when his stay in the intensive care unit went from days to weeks to more than two months. In pain and incapacitated with wires and tubes running to and from him, rather than being belligerent and resentful, I remember seeing him mouth the words "thank you" when offered ice chips to quench his thirst. There is little wonder that his favorite nurse – someone who was not fortunate enough to know him when he was well – was among the most grief-stricken to visit after his death.

As mourners – hundreds of them – passed by at the funeral home there were comments about his optimism, his laugh, his common sense, his ability to tell a story for seemingly any situation.

There were chuckles over his practical jokes and, of course, talk of his euchre playing. How he loved to play that game.

There were tears, lots and lots of them. And there will be many

Russ Mewhorter

more. But how comforting it is to know how much others think of your family. I had grandparents die 17 years ago in an automobile accident and I still have people tell me what a fine couple they were. It is nice to know that others remember. The same will be true of my father-in-law. People will remember.

He will be remembered through his involvement in the Lions and the Grange and his church. He will be remembered because he was a member of the hospital board and was a township trustee and was the secretary of the Wyandot County Fair Board for years. But the biggest reason he will be remembered is because he genuinely liked people. You can tell when a human being likes people. You can always tell.

For Norris Alfred, slower was better

Steve Zender
May 29, June 5, 1996

N orris Alfred must have been some character. How I wish I could have met the man who featured a bespectacled snail on the masthead of his newspaper and used the slogan, "Slower is Better." He owned the Polk Progress, a little weekly in Nebraska.

Unfortunately I was unfamiliar with Mr. Alfred's work until after he died last December. A tribute to him, along with a couple of his columns, appeared in Grassroots Editor, a publication for weekly newspapers. It was a fitting place to find out about the man. Norris Alfred was apparently about as "grassroots" as you could get.

I wrote about the Nebraska publisher and was surprised when an Alvada woman, Mrs. Joseph Saltzman, called to tell me Norris Alfred's nephew (also named Norris Alfred) was her son-in-law, lives in nearby Vanlue, and teaches in the Riverdale school system.

I have since received a letter from Ted Alfred, the publisher's brother (and the father of Norris) who had read my column and paid me what I considered a huge compliment by saying, "you surely seem a kindred soul." He sent me the eulogy he had written for his brother, using many of Norris' writings.

Norris Alfred was an artist, as well as a writer, and his brother said Norris admitted to originally wanting to increase the value of The Polk Progress, sell it, and return to painting. "But his love for Polk grew," his brother said, as he saw his town and "community concepts ... threatened by trends in the country he deplored. So he stayed and became outspoken and aggressive, where he felt it was needed, while keeping his sense of humor and respect for human sensitivities."

Norris Alfred had a distrust of the pace of technological progress and the rapidity of change," his brother wrote.

"Slower is Better," decided Norris Alfred.

Alfred didn't rush to upgrade his newspaper with the latest in technology, but he was way ahead of his time. We rush toward the 21st Century worrying about huge chicken and hog "factories," but Alfred was railing about bigness in farming a couple of decades ago. The Farm Bureau says huge farm operations are inevitable, he noted. "The myth of inevitability is always proposed by so-called pragmatists when practicality rots social fabric, endangers the environment, introducing previously unknown risks to daily life," he wrote.

In a Sept. 6, 1979, column he noted: "A Catholic church in Iowa is organizing its farm community members in opposition to bigness in farming and we applaud the attempt while wanting to write the priest and describe the first aid treatment for head wounds caused by butting them against a brick wall."

Another Alfred comment: "When we voiced some concern of odors from a confinement hog operation, we were told not to complain, it was the smell of money. 'It is not,' we replied, 'it is the smell of hog shit.'"

Alfred said that "Progress is a myth propounded by hucksters who claim they can detect it in bigger, faster, higher. Progress is confused with change to the extent that every change is declared progress as we journey from worse to better while accumulating much, more, most."

Our newspaper has all the trappings that suggest we are succumbing to the technological progress Norris Alfred worried about in his musings. We have computers, laser printers, scanners, digital cameras, faxes, modems. But I think he would be pleased to note that we keep a healthy amount of "distrust" of what is known as "progress."

For Norris Alfred, slower was better

Those who believe that "Slower is Better," don't necessarily have anything against changes in the world. Norris Alfred's brother relates finding this underlined passage written by Loren Eiseley next to his brother's bed: "I have dropped sunflower seed on stony mesa tops and planted cactus in alpine meadows amidst bluebells and the sound of water. I have sowed Northern seeds South and Southern seeds North and crammed acorns into the most unlikely places. You can call it a hobby if you like. In a small way I am a world changer and leaving my mark on the future."

An ode
to Ade

Gene Logsdon
May 6, 1981

I t was disconcerting, to say the least, to see Adrian Rall in the hospital. Ade, as we call him out here in Canady thistle country south of Upper Sandusky, is my first cousin once removed, whatever that means. I've never been able to figure out "once-removed" cousins. Which one got removed from the other?

Anyhow, we have all come to think of Ade as an enduring part of our neighborhood, like the hills along Warpole Creek and St. James Run. Like the Canadian thistles. You can whack Canady thistles down all day, all week, all summer, and if you turn your back a half hour, they grow right back up and grin at you. And so with Ade. He gets down but never out. And this time was no exception. It wasn't a week later he was back on his feet again.

One of the first times Ade "got down," his back ached so bad he could hardly walk. It got so he couldn't carry a sack of feed on his shoulder out to the hog trough as was his habit every morning. But the hogs had to be fed. He found that he could hook a big bucket to a V-belt looped around his neck, and carry feed that way. One morning on his tortuous way through the hog lot, the pain got too bad. He blanked out and fell. Louella, his wife, found him there. Recalls Ade with a grin, "It's lucky I had the feed with me for the hogs to eat. Otherwise, they might have eaten me." The doctors said that Ade's farming days were over. That's been more than 10 years ago and he's still going.

But seeing him in that hospital bed gave me a weird feeling. There he lay, all cleaned up, more or less helpless, wired up to one of those heart monitors, looking pale. For a man his age – someplace in the 80s – his skin looked remarkably youthful, his arms more muscular and wiry than a man half his age. I knew he was going to get well. About all he wanted to talk about was when in the mutter-mutter-mutter were they going to let him out of there.

But I couldn't get used to seeing him there in bed. I have in my mind an unforgettable vision of Ade out of one of my earlier, clear memories. He stands high on a strawstack, swarthy, lean, tough as whang leather, shaping the stack as the straw swirls out around him from the cannon-like blower of the threshing machine. Apart from the drama inherent in that scene, I remember it well because Ade always wore a big red bandanna handkerchief up over his face to keep some of the dust out of his nose and lungs. With his wide-brimmed straw hat, he looked to my five-year-old eyes like a cowboy. I had no idea he was my first cousin once removed. I thought he was Tom Mix.

As I grew up, Ade remained a sort of hero to me, because he never fell, like I did, for all the advice farmers were told they had to follow to be successful. Ade made money for Ade, not for the bankers and the agribusinessmen. He never farmed big, just well, and used the money he saved to buy other farms which he rented out. He kept horses long after horses were supposed to be inefficient. His machinery was always about 20 years behind the times. He had no outside job. He didn't borrow money, he lent it. He did not buy every silly gadget a proper farmer was supposed to buy. He led a disciplined life close to home, happy to be tied to his farm because he was a real farmer.

But money is not the sign of success. The successful man is the one who has found a way to do the work in life he really wants to do, and then is able to do it for the longest possible time. Ade loves his farming, and he has continued to farm for nearly two decades after most men retire. That to me is true success.

The big things in life are the little things

For many years in my earlier life, my 6:30 alarm clock was Ade calling his sheep. I got to love that sound: A high, wavering, penetrating, long-drawn cry of Shuuuuuuupeeeeeee, the second syllable dropping a note and tapering off echoing over the hills along Warpole Creek. Ade thinks he may have to get rid of his sheep and retire all the way "one of these days," but I've got a hunch he'll keep them as long as he can walk. But when the time comes, I'm not going to let his song die. I've got a few sheep and I've been practicing Ade's call. I'm going to keep it ringing over these hills for another generation. If there are any farm children still raised in the country around here in the next 30 years, which I doubt, I want them to wake up in the morning hearing something besides the drone of airplanes spraying poisons on the land.

Taps for
Bill Wood

Gene Logsdon
Feb. 17, 1993

This is probably the shortest column I ever will write. Then again in a way, it may be the longest.

There must be two or three hundred people in this county that I would like to give a little speech to. It would go like this. "Just by being who and what you are, you are a source of joy and inspiration to me. I really like you." But few of us ever do that. We wait until the person dies and then we say it.

I thought most of the night of what I could say to pay tribute to Woody. Once I wrote an article about him in a business magazine. I asked him what advice he had for other businesspeople. "Never retire," he said without hesitation. "There's nothing more boring than to wake up in the morning without something worthwhile to do." He tried to retire, then came back and built a brand new restaurant. That made him a giant in my eyes.

The big things in life are the little things

But what could I say that reflected the community's feelings, not just mine. And then it came to me. I didn't have to say anything. All I had to do was put into words a little incident that happened when he died, and that would immortalize the man who fed us all for so many years.

Here's what happened:

Jim Barnes was eating at Woody's when the word came that Bill had died. It was not unusual that Jim was there because he was a regular patron. While everyone, misty eyed, groped for something to say, or looked away, or down at their plates, Jim got up without a word, all on his own, walked out the door, across the parking lot, and lowered Bill's beloved flag to half-mast.

When he turned to walk back into the restaurant, there were some of the waitresses standing at the window, tears in their eyes, their thumbs up.

Bill Wood

Wyandot wonder

Gene Logsdon
Aug. 5, 1987

Herman Schoenberger is another of the natural wonders of Wyandot County, as all who know him attest. If he is not an electrical genius, then neither was Edison. Anyway, he tells this story about himself and his unceasing battle against the system.

Herman went into a store to pay a bill. I'll not say what store because it really doesn't matter, but it was not one in our county. When he announced his intention, the clerk who waited on him could not find the bill. The search finally revealed that it was in the outgoing mail, which had not been picked up yet. So the clerk fetched the bill and presented it to Herman, who pulled out his check book and wrote out a check for the prescribed amount.

When he handed the check over, the clerk said she needed his driver's license to verify the check. Herman refused. "You were going to send the bill in the mail and get my check back without looking at my driver's license, so why do you have to look at it now?" he argued. "It's our policy," said the clerk. "Well then give me the check back and send me your bill, if you want to be that way about it."

The big things in life are the little things

A second and eventually a third clerk were called into action, but Herman was equal to all three of them. He, by heaven, would not show them his driver's license because that was stupid. They decided they would settle by using any credit card he had for verification. "But I'm not buying on credit and never do," Herman said stoutly. Finally, as an amused crowd gathered, he admitted to having a credit card, and consented to letting them use it so long as it was quite clear he was paying the bill now.

That settled, Herman stepped back and grinned, pointing at the little sign each clerk was wearing, which stated that if the clerk did not ask the customer to buy some soap that was on special, the customer would get some free. "And by the way," Herman said, "you owe me some soap I believe."

The clerks glared at him, but good sports, they agreed. Herman, by now feeling a little ashamed of himself for causing such a problem, decided to buy some more of the soap to go along with the freebie, just to show his good will. He got out his check book again. "Tell you what," he suggested, "I'll just write out another check in the amount of the soap and the bill that I just paid, and you can give me back the first check." Can't do that, he was informed. Got to have a check for every transaction. "But all you have to do is hand back the old check – you've got the cash register open – and take the new one for both items. Just saves you paperwork." For the next few minutes the two checks passed back and forth getting a bit mutilated in the process, until Herman tore his name off the bottom of the first one he had written. That settled the matter, more or less. The clerk had only the second check. Out of habit she looked at it and said: "Can I see your driver's license, please?" Herman stared in unrepentant disbelief. "You really want to go through all that again?" She capitulated. Herman had won one against the system. Hooray.

From one of his friends

Steve Zender
June 23, 1993

I wrote a eulogy for a friend. But I couldn't say those words aloud at the funeral. After losing too many good friends too early, I knew it would be impossible to control the lump in the throat, the quiver in the voice and the tears in the eyes.

Emotions are especially difficult to contend with when the friend you have lost is Rick Miller. Thousands of tributes have been written that extol the love of family, winning smiles, pleasing personalities and overcoming adversity, but in Rick's case, all the compliments are true. When mourners say "everyone liked this man," it is not an idle statement. It is a sincere statement of fact.

Toni says Rick worried about having too many wrinkles in his face for a 47-year-old man. "Those are laugh lines," she told him. And she meant that, too. Every crease could be traced to a smile.

Not that all in the Millers' life went as they would have liked. Over the years there were numerous difficulties, some now, in retrospect, as trivial as a flooded basement or as repairable as Toni's broken arm from a fall on the ice. Other problems were much more serious and potentially tragic: A home burned to the ground; a young son was hospitalized; a daughter seriously injured in a terrible car crash. And in the early days, Rick battled a weakness for alcohol. But he wrestled that problem to the ground and beat it, for the sake of Toni and Eric and Michael and Megan. For the sake of his friends and himself.

Through all the adversity, Rick Miller found plenty to smile about: when he heard complaints from his friends that he won too much of their money on the golf course; when Megan accused him of getting his hair cut too short at all the wrong times – like the day of homecoming; winning or losing when he played euchre. There were smiles even when his beloved Cleveland Indians would lose once again. He'd adjust the ever-present baseball cap and warn, "Wait till next year."

His love of coaching might have matched his fondness for the Indians and the Browns. Year after year he suggested to Toni that this might be his last as head baseball coach at Carey. But she knew better and so did the rest of us. There would be good prospects on the horizon; or a regional tournament appearance; or a good regular season record to spur him on to yet another year. We all knew he would coach forever.

Rick Miller

90

From one of his friends

We also expected, especially considering the longevity of his father's family, that we'd some day see Rick Miller as an old man, if we were lucky enough to still be alive.

We teased him about his driving speed – or more correctly, his lack of it. There was the regular travel time and then there was how long it would take Rick to get there. Like his driving, we expected Rick's life to be a relaxed trip that would go on and on. But for reasons we don't comprehend, Rick reached his destination much more quickly than any of us expected. And for our own loving but selfish reasons, it was much sooner than we would have liked.

There are many lessons we could learn from this friend of ours. But maybe the most important knowledge to be gained is to remember why people liked this man so much. Understand that and maybe more of those creases in our own face will come from smiles.

Death of
a hero

Gene Logsdon
April 13, 1988

Jerome Frey, of near Kirby, died a couple of weeks ago. I don't know whether to call him my best teacher or my hero. He was the hero of the whole Kirby community to be sure, and if the world knew him as we did, he would be honored right up there with our nation's greatest.

I had to travel thousands of miles, live in eight different places in six different states, spend half a lifetime in classrooms and libraries and listen at the knees of scientists and artists, to learn what Jerome Frey just naturally knew: that the greatest work people can do is to manage their own selves, families, homes and neighborhoods virtuously. If they can't do that, then they can't manage any other part of the world either. And if they did manage their own affairs properly, then the rest of the world would take care of itself.

Jerome was too kindly to enjoy criticizing others, but he would often shake his head and say, "It is no wonder this country is getting into such a fix. People are trying to run things whose own personal affairs are in a terrible mess." He had another observation I have used often in my writing: "A small community can always manage better than a large one because in a small place, everyone knows who the idiots are and don't appoint them to positions of responsibility. The only time there's a problem is when newcomers drift in who sound smart but aren't. They cause problems until they are found out and move on. The reason places like Columbus and Washington are screwed up is because that's where the drifters all finally move to."

I divide the world anymore between nurturers and parasites. People who build and people who tear down. People who produce and people who only consume. People who save and people who waste. Jerome Frey was a nurturer. He was a farmer all his life, but realized that good farming was not very profitable in itself, because you have to return to the soil what you take from it to keep it fertile. Rather than plunder the soil, and use the ill-gained profits to plunder other farmers of their land, Jerome, from the very beginning, did more than just farm. And he taught his sons and daughters to do likewise.

When he was young and "only" farming, he also was offering other services to farmers, like cleaning cloverseed, running a thresher, operating a sawmill. In the winter he found a lucrative sideline – hauling ice from farm ponds to Kirby's seven saloons. Later, he started a hardware business, a lumber business, a construction business, a grocery, and put his sons and daughters in charge of them. And when his son in charge of the grocery suffered bad health, Jerome pitched in way past retirement time and ran the store himself, not because he needed the money, but because he hated to see Kirby without a grocery.

Jerome was smart. If there would have been a gifted-child program in his day, he would have been in it and probably have had his head filled with nonsense, and gone off to college to become a white-collar broccoli-brain conniving for tax-financed tenure and retirement at 55.

But Jerome was **truly** smart, which means he could work with his hands, not just his mouth. He could build or make anything and he taught his children they could too. He developed a tradition of self-reliance in his community. Today his grandchildren, learning from fathers, mothers and grandparents, **believe** they can do anything they need to do, and by hickory, as Jerome would say, they do it. They don't whine around that they should be getting higher salaries for lesser work. They work longer – two jobs if they have to – and build themselves houses in their spare time while the whiners are out playing golf.

The big things in life are the little things

Jerome was the shrewdest leader I ever watched in action. The first time I met him, he and his strapping young sons came to build a barn for my father – back in the '50s. The boys were obviously in charge, and at first I wondered who the older man was, sort of off by himself nailing a door together. As with all the enterprises he started, he knew enough to stay in the background, to suppress his own ego for the good of family solidarity. He told me once that young people have to be free to make a few mistakes. And even the door he was making, he used to teach me a lesson. "You know," he said, "in this hurry-up world we live in now, it's not supposed to pay to build a door like I'm doing." He winked, "But then I'm not high-priced union labor either, and this is scrap wood."

Jerome loved music. He understood it as the language of the soul and that people who sing or learn to play musical instruments can enjoy one of life's greatest pleasures, and spend very little money in the process.

And I guess that is what I admired most in him – his simplicity. He enjoyed so much being a nurturer, a leader, a saver. Seeing his family and his community prosper even when the rural economy was supposed to be bad, prospering precisely because he had taught them how to live to weather bad times, was satisfaction enough for him. He liked to have a nice car, but he seldom traveled. Went to Florida once, he told me, and nearly froze to death. Asked a few months ago if there was anything or anywhere he'd like to go, he at first said no. Just wanted to be around home. Wasn't there anything he'd like to see before he died? He thought a little bit and said, "Well, I guess I'd like to watch a plow turn over rich dirt once more."

His sons and grandsons hauled his coffin from the funeral at the Kirby church to the cemetery with Junior's horses and wagon, and many of us walked along behind. It had been a long time since I saw horse-slobber spattered on the road. And even longer since I've seen tears falling behind wagon wheels.

But, by hickory, Jerome, we are going to make sure you did not teach the lessons of life in vain. The torch has been passed on not just to your children, but to your grandchildren, and that is the key. I saw it blazing in their tear-filled eyes at your funeral. They are going out and buying their little farms, like you taught them they must do. And building or repairing their little houses, and passing on to their children the self-reliance you inspired, without which this country is going to go completely to hell. They are building their little workshops, and minding their little stores, and starting their little businesses, and working like dogs wherever they have to, to carve out their places in the community.

I was trying to tell a friend from afar about these wonderful, salt-of-the-earth people who, like their kind all over America, do not get the credit they deserve for maintaining the stable, morally responsible, self-sufficient neighborhoods that are still left, and my friend chuckled. "But these people are the ones who are going to survive the collapse that's coming. They will be the builders of the new world." If so, there ought to be a statue of Jerome Frey somewhere to honor the people who will be the next saviours of mankind.

The Cookie
Lady throws
a party

Gene Logsdon
July 7, 1983

B erenice Kail, our neighbor, better known hereabouts as the Cookie Lady, celebrated her 85th birthday last week with a party. It was her first birthday party ever and she was afraid no one would come, underestimating the Wyandot Countian's love for a free lunch. It looked for awhile like the whole county would show up at the Cookie Lady's lovely old farmstead. No one knows how she does it, but the Cookie Lady not only bakes cookies for half the people in Mifflin Township, but she keeps half a million flowers blooming prodigiously around her home, too.

Some of us figured on gorging on the Cookie Lady's cookies all afternoon, but even she has her limits. At 85, she had the Von Steins cater the party. The Von Steins are another favorite topic of this column and that leaves me with a small problem. If I say I missed the cookies, Gladys might be secretly miffed, and if I say I didn't miss the cookies, Berenice might decide not to bake any more for me. So following my life rule, "Always Be Friends With The Cook," I will say that I have not been catered with a finer cake before, just as I have on other occasions, not been treated with a finer

The Cookie Lady throws a party

cookie.

All kinds of interesting people came to the party. I suddenly realized that a surprising number of them had figured one way or another in this column. Bill Dyviniak was there, from Buffalo, N.Y. He is the reason I got to know the Cookie Lady even though she and I had been nodding neighbors for years. You know the story, and it has been told and retold in Ohio Magazine, Guideposts and more recently by Paul Harvey on his national radio program. Years ago, Bill was flying over Wyandot County when a storm hit and he made a forced landing on a strip of pasture that appeared miraculously as he came plummeting out of the storm-ridden clouds.

The strip of pasture just happened to have been reserved by Kail's son, John, for his landing strip when he would come home from the Korean War. John never came home, his plane shot down in battle. Bill Dyviniak has ever since kept a windsock hanging on the Kail barn in memory and in gratitude, and has become like a son to Berenice. The story still makes me cry so I don't tell it too often.

Ann Goodman (Mrs. Wilson Goodman) was there and I have to tell you a story about her. She should be elected president of the U.S., or at least appointed ambassador to Russia. She really knows how to handle the opposition. Readers of this column know that Ann and I have had a polite historical disagreement. She traces her ancestry back to Colonel William Crawford, our county's only Revolutionary War hero. One of her keenest interests in life is researching Crawford's history and shedding honor upon his memory.

Then along comes this smart aleck columnist with innuendoes suggesting that Crawford got what he deserved when the Indians burned him at the stake. The typical reaction to a smart aleck columnist is to write a letter to the editor declaring that he is an idiot and a jackass as some worthy members of our community have done. But not Ann. She has real class. And she thought that columnists were reasonable folk who just didn't have the facts in hand. She invited me to her home where I was met with a stack of books nine feet tall, all purporting to show that Crawford was of blameless and inviolable character. When this did not move the smart aleck columnist, proving he was surely a jackass and an idiot, she still did not lose her patience. She knew my weakness. She invited me to her home once again where she and Wilson treated my wife and me to one of the most delicious dinners I've ever enjoyed – along with an interesting slide show about Crawford's importance to history. What can I do but capitulate? After such

97

kindness, dare I ever again say anything mean and nasty about that old squaw cha . . . ahem, that is that great Revolutionary War hero William Crawford?

Drs. Rhoads and Solacoff, longtime recipients of the Cookie Lady's cookies, were there. Doc Solacoff's first two initials are K.K., which, as I reported previously, stand for King Kong. But Berenice thinks they stand for Kookie Kruncher, which seems more likely.

Florence was there. I never remember her last name, but she's from Shaker Heights and I've enjoyed a delightful visit with her at the Kails before. Her husband has served important positions with Standard Oil and I was looking forward to meeting him, one of my ambitions in life being to punch a Standard Oil executive in the nose. But he (I can't remember his first name either) and Florence are such nice people. Standard Oil can't be all bad. Florence, in her usual jolly way, had a great joke to tell. There's this rooster, see, standing there with his comb drooping way down over his face. Another rooster is saying to him, "Why so crestfallen?"

If I could remember names better, I could turn this into one of those juicy gossip columns. But actually I didn't hear any juicy gossip for once. Just a nice Sunday afternoon in honor of a grand lady, and all the neighbors sitting in the yard wondering why we don't do this sort of thing more often.

So long, Punch

Gene Logsdon
June 7, 1995

If anyone should be called Mr. Upper Sandusky, Kenny McClain, whom we all called Punch, would be at the top of my list. At times, the line of people who filed tearfully past his coffin stretched all the way out of Lucas Funeral Home, halfway to S. Sandusky Avenue in both the afternoon and evening visitations. Punch knew everybody, and he could not mention a person without tracing his or her lineage back two or three generations. His infectious grin and buoyant spirit were the standard attractions of Upper Sandusky.

I loved to ride around Wyandot County with him because he had a tale to tell about nearly every house or farm we would pass. He savored the life of this county like no one else I know. If he had been a writer, what a book about us he could have written. But he was a builder. I would guess that he built or worked on a fourth of the houses in and around Upper over the years. Maybe more.

The big things in life are the little things

When he built our house, we gave him a rough drawing of what we had in mind, and this mostly self-taught builder went to work. We employed no official architect and never drew up a standard blueprint, much to the horror of people who think such conventions are absolutely necessary. I knew he'd do it right. I'd worked with him in earlier years in the Soil Conservation Service where he taught me how to survey, how to work up a topographical map, how to profile a drainage ditch to grade, how to run a ditcher, all of which Don Hall had taught him. But neither Punch nor I could qualify for the salary that an educated SCS worker made. We had not been properly trained in a cowlidge (one of my first lessons in the farce of the college racket).

Punch threw the best rise ball of any fastpitch softball pitcher I ever batted against. He was strong as an ox and fearless. My favorite story about him happened south of Columbus where we were putting in a tile drainage system on a farm of Ward Walton's far-flung empire. Punch ran the ditcher and several of what were called hillbillies before political correctness (they boasted that they were hillbillies and most of them were fine people) were laying tile behind the ditcher (all by hand in those days). One of these workers also boasted that he carried a knife of which he was inordinately proud, and liked to remind us that he knew how to use it.

One day, probably after a snort of moonshine (these fellows had some of the best whiskey I have ever tasted – smooth as plum juice and crystal clear) got a little muleheaded about laying tile fast enough to keep up with the ditcher, and Punch got on him for it. "Don't get smart with me," the man said, "unless you want to get a good look at my knife." Punch laughed, grabbed him by the seat of the pants and the scruff of the neck, and threw him clean across the tile ditch **and** a four-foot high pile of dirt on the other side of it. Punch made some pointed observations about what the guy could do with his knife and then he turned around and said, "That's the way with guys like that. All shit and wind."

Punch and I disagreed about the county's retention and expansion plans, but unlike those snobnoses in Upper who refuse to speak to me because I dare question their uppercrust expertise, Punch would come out here to my office and we'd argue.

Punch was plenty smart, but he had no sense of the written word or what I was trying to do with it. He marvelled over how fast I could type and seemed to believe that fast typing was the secret of my being able to make a living from writing. He was a good businessman and had a canny sense of safe, sane economics. As I'd tell him, if he were in charge of expansion and retention, then I'd be for it.

Once when we were young and money was dear, I went with Punch to Crow Motors where he had spotted a used car he knew was in good shape. Finally he got the price down to $1,200 as I recall and the salesman commenced to discuss financing the purchase. Punch opined that if he could pay cash, the price ought to drop a little more, say to $1,000. The salesman agreed with that, thinking Punch was joking, as he often was. At that point, Punch whipped out a roll of cash from his pocket and counted out 10 $100 bills before our astonished eyes.

He also had a good sense of human nature. The most surprising thing he ever said to me, and I guess it's okay to repeat it now that he is gone, was about the instability of marriages these day. "There's too many couples sitting too long in bars staring at each other's spouses," he said. "I suspect the private club bars are one of the main causes of marriage problems in Upper."

We miss you, Punch. There's a big empty place in town that your great gift of common sense once filled to overflowing.

Kenny "Punch" McClain

A fine
doctor and
a fine man

Gene Logsdon
Oct. 18, 1978

E very time I start plinking away on this typewriter, which is almost
daily, I breathe a thankful sigh for C.B. Schoolfield, Upper
Sandusky's long-time family doctor. Were it not for him, my right
forefinger would be missing down to the first knuckle and I'd have a deuce
of a time hitting the y-u-h-j-n-m keys.

In 1961 my finger got caught in an argument between a wagon
tongue and a tractor drawbar. By the time Dr. Schoolfield attended to it, the
finger did not look worth the bother of being attended to. But rather than
complete the amputation, which seemed the practical solution, Schoolfield
sewed the fingertip back on. It's still with me and I do 't ave to t pe se te ces
t at look like t is.

Clarence Blakeney Schoolfield is retiring this week, and those of us
who depend on him for our doctoring are going to miss him sorely. To me,
he's one of the last truly genuine doctors. Many doctors today are professional skiers, golfers, fishermen, skydivers, hunters, scuba divers and race car
fanatics who practice a little medicine in their spare time. Schoolfield is a

full-time doctor. You don't have to wait until Tuesday-Wednesday-Thursday to get sick. You can get sick on Saturday even, and Schoolfield will be around to take care of you. Just last week he opened his office to handle an emergency on Sunday morning. **Sunday morning!** "This is the end of an era," said the mother who had called him for assistance. "I don't think we'll ever enjoy the luxury again of a doctor who will see us on Sunday morning."

You didn't have to have an appointment to see Schoolfield. You just walked in and waited your turn. And you never had to wait as long as when you make an appointment to see a doctor. Nor did he charge what he could have charged. People who were really poor, though doing the best they could, he charged little.

D r. Schoolfield started his career in the coal fields of West Virginia, taking over his father's practice. But where his father rode a horse, Schoolfield equipped his car with oversized balloon tires that would roll over the ruts and trails and creek bottoms without hanging up. He delivered babies by the light of fireplaces. Without the help of $300-per-hour anesthesiologists, he drafted family members to help out, worrying all the while near the open flame that the ether might explode. People recovered just as fast without Blue Cross. The mountaineers seldom offered to pay him money, but when he climbed into his car to leave, he'd find a fat roasted hen or a bottle of good moonshine on the seat.

Upper Sandusky was pretty tame after that. For years Schoolfield traveled our country roads in an old Plymouth he refused to trade because no snowdrift seemed able to stop it. To this day he has a hard time believing people really get snowbound. He never did. He never dared to.

If you know whom to ask, you will hear wonderful stories of Schoolfield's courage and dedication as a doctor. He'd probably dismiss the stories if I asked him about them, because those who work with him say he never takes credit for remarkable recoveries. He will only say he does "everything he can" and then some power greater than any doctor's skill seems to take over. But there are people alive and healthy in this county who would be dead were it not for Schoolfield's tenacity, even after other doctors had given up.

Perhaps the most poignant incident, many years ago, concerned one battle with death at birth the doctor lost. The mother had known a particularly difficult time conceiving and carrying the child and its birth was a very special event of joy. But through nobody's fault except nature's the little boy died at birth – I'm told the only baby Schoolfield ever "lost." But the doctor would not give up, trying to breath life back into the little body. He finally had to be almost physically taken away. One of the nurses there said it was the only time she had ever seen tears in Schoolfield's eyes.

He has a reputation for being gruff in the traditional doctor's "tough but oh so gentle" way. Seeing the raw reality of suffering and death almost daily, he has little patience with those who believe they are sick because they haven't any other way to entertain themselves. Busy people don't get sick very much, he has sometimes observed. On the other hand,

Doctor C.B. Schoolfield

he can get exasperated by people like me who think they can cure themselves and then come, too late, to seek his aid. A friend of mine says he went to Schoolfield, told him what sickness was afflicting him and what medicine he was taking. Schoolfield stared at him a second or two and then asked, "Are you going to do the doctoring, or do you want me to?"

Like other honest, disciplined professionals, Schoolfield has only contempt for government regulations that serve little purpose but to provide salaries for minor bureaucrats. In earlier years, the onslaught of useless and duplicating forms to fill out made him furious. (Some say he's mellowed in recent years.) When he was feeling particularly irked, he liked to call over to the courthouse about 2:30 in the afternoon and in honey-sweet tones introduce himself with "Good morning." Or say in mock surprise, "Oh, are you still in your office this late in the day?"

He can have an outrageous sense of humor. A new secretary was horrified one day when the good doctor dismissed an elderly female patient (now deceased) with nasty remarks as the patient shuffled out of the examining room. "Get out of here old woman and quit your whining. You're not sick and you're wasting my time when I've got real patients to see." Then he grinned wickedly at the shocked secretary and returned to his desk. In a few minutes he ducked back out and told the secretary, "One thing you should know. That old woman can read lips, but she's deafer than a post."

Schoolfield is deeply devoted to his wife and family, a shining example in these "modern" times when a shoddy entertainment business would try to convince people such devotion isn't possible. One of the cruelest experiences of his life was spending the Second World War in the Pacific right during his daughters' best growing-up years.

He likes football – he played when he was in school. He played a high school game once with broken ribs. "I didn't dare tell anyone or my father would have taped me up and forbidden me to play. He follows the games today, particularly Ohio State. On Saturday afternoons when the flow of patients had let up, he used to listen to the games in his back room, sitting in a big stuffed chair. "Often he'd fall asleep because he'd been at the hospital or making house calls all night," recalls a secretary.

A community can't have too many men like Schoolfield, but having one is fortunate. What he has done for us would fill volumes. There's no way to thank him except maybe to emulate his example of forthrightness, gentlemanliness and dedication and pass it on to a younger generation.

We wish you well in your retirement, but we're gong to miss you, Doctor.

A special place for friends

Steve Zender
May 8, 1991

S till mourning the death of my very good friend Randy Smalley, who died a few short weeks ago, I now watch my daughter deal with the grief of losing someone close to her.

Nine-year-old kids aren't supposed to lose friends. They're supposed to jump and giggle – and Gail and Molly certainly did plenty of that together. That's what little girls are supposed to do. They are not supposed to die.

Most of us can only imagine the horror of losing a son or a daughter. But we know what it feels like to see others suffer their loss and we feel our throat tightening and the tears coming when we think about how we have lost something and someone important to ourselves and to our families.

We ask why. And, of course, there is no answer. No one can answer why. But we wonder anyway. Some turn to their religion for comfort; some find other ways to persevere. Time heals, they say, but it never returns us to the point from which we started. And, if we could, we'd stop time and change things. Just for a moment we'd change things. A tree would not fall; a traffic accident would be avoided. If only a few seconds from the past could

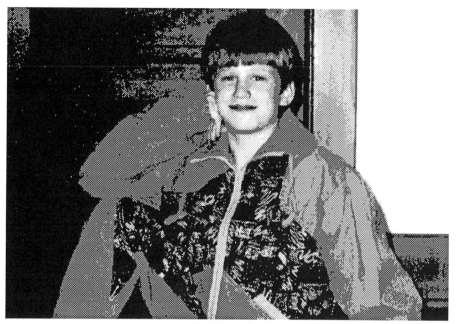

Gail Coppler

be grasped and manipulated, we would make things better. Like they were before.

But we can't change a thing. We go on as best we can, wondering why, all the while knowing that much smarter people have wondered the same question and received no answer.

Little children, I'm told, accept these things much better than adults. Those who are used to helping people handle terrible losses explain that if children are allowed to express their grief, they can deal with the loss. Molly said even the boys cried last week at school.

Maybe the reason adults have so much trouble understanding death is that we grow more selfish as we grow older. We have plans and we expect our friends to be there. Even if we accept the idea of our friends "being in a better place," we mourn for our own loss. When the golf season begins, I expect my teammates to be there. And I miss them if they're not.

Thankfully, children learn quickly that accepting a death does not mean forgetting a friend. Gail was the star player on her soccer team. There was a special place reserved for her on the bench last Saturday. Molly said she even sat on Gail's lap once. There will always be a special place for friends, even after they are gone.

Goodbye, old Pal

Steve Zender
Final chapter of "The Commander of Carey"
Ohio Magazine, November 1994

I remember the day George Henry Bish died. It was a beautiful, crisp, blue-sky day with a blinding sun. It was one of those September days so clear that everything before it seemed out of focus. George, now 82, was shuffling back from Fritz Cassel's office, where he had just received his $5 allowance.

The Commander was heading toward the coffee shop to sit with Bobby Donelson and the boys. George knew he had the right-of-way at the crosswalk near Ray Peiffer's office on Findlay Street. It was with this knowledge that he headed across the street, looking neither right nor left after he started. At approximately 10:02 a.m., the glaring sun, an old man's shuffle, an automobile, and another old man's eyesight combined for one terrible instant.

George was hit full-force by the moving vehicle. His false teeth – those damned things that never did fit – went flying. George came out of his shoes, such was the impact, and he crashed to the pavement, his head violently striking the ground. He loosened his grip on his black satchel. It lay on the ground, the eagle decal looking skyward.

Police and emergency medical personnel were there in an instant. And they already knew the eventual outcome of this accident. George Henry Bish was going to die.

Police Chief Bill Swartz tried to comfort Harold Howard, 88, the driver of the vehicle. And, at the accident scene, with tears in his eyes, he gathered up George Henry's belongings: his shoes, his black satchel – it would lay in the coffin with him on the day of his funeral – and his teeth. Bill patted George Henry's arm as the EMS people prepared to load their pal into the ambulance for the hopeless race to Blanchard Valley Hospital.

George never regained consciousness. At 8:44 that evening, Sept. 18, 1989, the life of Commander George Henry Bish came to an end.

It was a Monday, our busiest day in the newspaper office, and I remember Linda Kin telling me George had just been in a bad accident. I didn't think much about it at first. George had fallen down stairs, had an operation, banged himself up in crashes on the sidewalk. But he always bounced back. Then she added, "They said there was no way he was going to make it."

The office was quiet, as if everyone was trying to contemplate a week without George Henry Bish. Today was the day he'd deliver the church bulletin from yesterday's service at Christ Lutheran Church. I suppose the bulletins were still in his black bag the day he was buried.

I thought about George, as a disheveled old man wearing white gloves, rising, tapping his director's batton on the pew in front of him, and leading the congregation in song. I could hear him pronounce the name of his favorite conductor. "John Philip Soosie" is the way he said it. People called him Pal, Commander, John Philip – the names were interchangeable – but they all had special meaning in reference to George Henry Bish.

There was no immediate family to mourn George Henry's passing, but there was an entire community.

Tom Wedge called. I hadn't talked to him in years, since he sold his sporting goods store in Carey and moved away. "Steve?" he asked. I recognized his voice at once, even though it might have been the first time he had ever called me by my first name. "Is it true about Pal?"

I told him it was. There was a long silence. "I loved that old guy," he said quietly.

The big things in life are the little things

I scrapped my weekly newspaper column and wrote another for the week. I told about how George Henry brought the best out in people and how he always urged me to "write my life's story, pal."

"If I ever do," I wrote, "it will contain stories about a lot of heroes from Carey, Ohio."

Near George's casket were pictures and mementos. There was George with a woman on his lap; George with a birthday cake; George wearing a sombrero; George in his white gloves and baton; George in his military outfit. There were flag pins and buttons.

The Rev. Paul DeMoss gave an upbeat eulogy. He talked about how George did the best with what he had. He talked about George's love of people and his love of music. The congregation sang three songs, including "Battle Hymn of the Republic," one of George's favorites.

Military rules wouldn't permit a 21-gun salute for this particular commander, but the VFW color guard was there at his graveside, standing at attention as George Henry Bish was laid to rest.

By school-time 1989, Carey's fear of losing its band director to a larger school had come to pass. Greg Taylor had married and moved on to Columbus. But Carey was lucky. Barbara Lumbrezer had proved to be an excellent replacement and the school band continued to be impressive.

It was May 1990, and the Carey band was again presenting its spring concert. Lumbrezer had displayed a remarkable memory by flawlessly introducing every single band member – from fifth grade to seniors – as they took the stage and received awards. She thanked the senior class for its cooperation during the transition period and for making her first year at Carey successful and enjoyable. The concert band was nearing the end of its performance when the director announced a special selection that

George Henry Bish

wasn't listed in the program.

The year before George Henry had been invited to conduct the band in "The Stars and Stripes Forever." To a novice eye like mine his peformance was flawless. John Philip Soosie left no doubt that he was thrilled with the opportunity. I can still see him bowing to the crowd before he stepped up on the podium, then bowing again, and again and again, as the packed auditorium erupted in a spontaneous, thunderous standing ovation at the conclusion. The band members arose to applaud their leader as he continued to take his bows.

Lumbrezer had never met the Commander but she had learned he was a special member of the community. Now, a year after his performance, she was saying the following number was presented in George Henry's memory.

The director walked from the stage. There was silence for a moment. And then the band began. The podium was empty as the wonderful sounds of "The Stars and Stripes Forever" filled the auditorium. I remembered how excited George Henry had been the year before and how proud I was of those young band kids when they stood and applauded him. I remembered the overwhelming ovation from the audience. And I smiled to myself, recalling all those bows George Henry made.

And then I cried. Not for George Henry Bish. If there's a heaven, John Philip Soosie has his white gloves on and has already elbowed his way to the front of the angelic choir. I cried for us. God, I was proud of our town and our people that night. But who, I wondered, would now remind us all of our humanity?

If we weren't all crazy, we would go insane

...Jimmy Buffett

If we weren't all crazy

Steve Zender
July 18, 1990

Ten of us made our annual trek last Friday to hear Jimmy Buffett in concert. This trip was special because we took The Country Rover along and I eagerly await his "cultural shock" column on this subject.

I'm writing about one of my singing heroes (Buffett, not Logsdon) because he often suggests what I've maintained for a long time: that we're all nuts. In one of his earliest songs, Buffett suggested, "If we weren't all crazy, we'd all go insane." His songs often marvel at the crazy things we do. Buffett has grown to wonder about this while traversing the world. I've grown to wonder about it by staying put in my home town of Carey, Ohio.

Buffett grew up (well, actually, he claims in song he is "growing older, but not up") in a different place and different circumstances than I did, but we were born in the same year. And I've read he was hooked, same as me, on the music of Harry Belafonte. It seems now only natural that I eventually became fascinated by Buffett's songs.

The big things in life are the little things

The name Jimmy Buffett usually evokes one of two reactions. People either have a puzzled look and ask, "Who?" Or they break out in song and tell you about the latest Hawaiian shirt they've bought.

It is as impossible to give a good description of a Buffett fan as it is to pin a label on the music he writes and sings. Fans range from cowboys to yuppies; from pre-teens to retirees. And his musical sound includes country and rock and many stops in between. He likes the music of the 1940s, for example, and some of that creeps into his music. A woman told me a young fan described his music as "island music." I suppose that explanation is as good as any.

See thousands of crazy Buffett fans – most of them dressed in tropical clothing and many (including us) in crazy hats – and there will be little doubt that this is some sort of a cult following. But a happy, harmless one, unless you count the number of drunks you see.

Fans know the words to the songs and they know when there is to be choreography. Buffett music is seldom on the radio and he's never won any sort of musical award, yet his fans flock to his concerts and buy up his records in impressive numbers. Parrots and palm trees and sharks and flamingos and ocean scenes make up Jimmy Buffett props and you'll see all that stuff at a concert. The crazier a hat, the better. I own a parrot hat (from head to tail, a couple of feet long; wingspan 18 inches or so) which is a hit with fellow fans. I loaned it to the Country Rover last week and he looked good.

If Buffett fans form a cult, just what is the message? I've thought about that, but pinning down an exact message from Buffett is like trying to pin down the exact sound of his music. Maybe the message is, "There is no message." But that's not quite right either. Forced to sum up what Buffett is saying, I suppose it would be this: "Relax. Don't get so excited. Tomorrow's another day. Chill out. You'll laugh about this in the morning. Don't make such a big deal out of this. Live and let live. Enjoy your stay. Dream a little."

Still, there is more to Buffett than that. There are songs about lost loves; concerns about the environment; nostalgic talks about the past; loving comments about family and friends, and the suggestion that you'd better live your life to the fullest. "I'd rather die while I'm living than live while I'm dead," Buffett sings.

I've heard people say that Buffett is getting more mellow as he ages (he's 43, which is a wonderful age, if you ask me!) but I'm not too sure. Maybe a little more mellow, but he's always had a mellow side, mixed in with some "in your face" liberalism. Naturally, I like that a lot.

If Buffett is preaching to his cult, his sermon is to enjoy your life because it's the only one you've got. I suppose he's as hypocritical about some things as the rest of us, but there is a refreshing honesty, too. He sticks to the music he likes, even though it means he probably won't get much play on the radio. On the other hand, he's not afraid of being a businessman. He has stores that sell all sorts of Buffett material and his shows are often sponsored by Corona beer. But Buffett the businessman disappears when he decides to take on an indifferent government or developers who he feels are ruining the environment in the Florida Keys.

Buffett's songs are considered "clean" by most modern-day standards, but he's also been the victim of censorship from time to time and that just adds grist for his mill. His concerts and many of his songs have that "just slightly out of control" reputation. I would imagine he has developed that very carefully. One of his song says, "I've read dozens of books about heroes and crooks and I learned much from both of their styles." And that's the way most of his fans look at him: part fearless leader; part pirate.

A well-placed cuss word here and there creeps into Jimmy's works and fans seem to give a high approval rating to that. In one of his regular numbers he sings, "There's been good times and riches and ..." pausing, the crowd finishes the sentence, "son-of-a-bitches." The crowd has, by its reaction, seen a lot of SOBs too.

Some folks would call Buffett irresponsible because of some of his songs. Others might figure that verses about a "Cheeseburger in Paradise" and volcanoes and coconut telegraphs and fish really aren't all that important. I imagine Jimmy would agree. But he could easily fill a few stadiums full of people who would argue that there are a lot of stuffed shirts in places like Washington, D.C., and New York City who are much more irresponsible and are doing work that is much less important.

If you can learn to relax and laugh in the face of life's heartaches, you've probably taken your first step toward becoming a Buffett fan. Learn some songs and go to a concert and you'll become a full-fledged fanatic. You'll be what is known in the language of Buffett as a Parrot Head. And always remember, "If we weren't all crazy, we would go insane."

Let's tour Wyandot County

Steve Zender
July 31, 1996

S till planning that trip through Historical Wyandot County?

Before you go crashing out the door, let me offer some background on the must-see stops.

Indian Mill. All tours of Wyandot County must start here, the most photographed, sketched and painted historical spot in Wyandot County. Indian Mill is located on the Sandusky River (a Polish river, originally spelled Sanduski). The original gristmill was built by the U.S. Government and given to the Wyandot Indians in 1820 "in appreciation of the Wyandot Indians' loyalty during the War of 1812." The government apparently stayed appreciative for a couple decades. Then, for some reason, the government became unappreciative and ran the Indians off to Kansas in 1841.

Battle Island. Really not an island, but the spot where Colonel William Crawford was defeated by the Indians. This was about the last time anything good happened to the Indians until they won the American League pennant in 1995.

The Battle Island monument was erected in 1926 by the Improved Order of the Red Men, a fraternal society made up of a bunch of white guys who swore to live by the "principles of Redmanism," which apparently had something to do with chewing tobacco.

Chief Tarhe. Born in 1742, the great Wyandot leader convinced the tribes to abide by the terms of the 1796 Treaty of Greenville, which is more than any white leader could do with his followers.

Tarhe is credited with bringing peace between the whites and the Indians but, of course, the whites didn't consider it true peace until they owned all the Wyandot's land and shipped them out.

Not known to many historians, Tarhe's full name is Shoulda Tarhe, which means, literally, in the language of the Wyandots, "Should have tarred and feathered the white, egotistical, cheating bigots when we had the chance."

**Erected in 1877 ...
and again in 1994.**

Parker Covered Bridge. Built in 1873. Burned in 1991. Rebuilt in 1993. Considered historically significant because for nearly 100 years it was held together entirely by graffiti.

Mission Church. Collective effort by whites, Indians and at least one black. Building the church enabled local leaders to feel good about themselves and say, "Okay, okay, we ran the Indians out of town, but at least Kansas is getting a bunch of Christians."

The big things in life are the little things

Joseph McCutchen. His friends called him Scutch. He operated the Overland Inn and was also a state legislator, but that doesn't necessarily mean he was all bad. Charles Dickens stayed at the Overland in 1843 and was overheard saying, "You know, this really is the worst of times."

Colonel William Crawford. A friend of George Washington, but then, who wasn't. Crawford was killed by the Delaware Indians on June 11, 1782, and has numerous monuments sprinkled around the area to prove it. There is one at a roadside park in Crawford; one on private ground along Tymochtee Creek; another newer monument across the creek, which looks exactly like the old monument on the other side of the creek. While historians can't decide on the exact location of Crawford's demise along Tymochtee Creek, sex experts leave no doubt about the monuments. All agree they look like phallic symbols. Hook a motor on that thing and you've got the world's largest vibrator. It is sometimes fondly called the Colonel Condom monument.

Tymochtee Creek. Tributary in Wyandot County, which means, in the Wyandot language, "Creek that runs past many monuments."

Crawford. This tiny village was once a settlement of the Delaware Indians. The infamous Simon Girty, who was said to have played a part in the death of Colonel Crawford, reportedly said to Indian leader Captain Pipe, "Wouldn't it be really cool to kill Crawford in a town named after him?"

So there you have it. We could travel down what was once called The Indian Trail, starting from that big tree near Upper Sandusky that was bent like an arrow, pointing the way toward Carey. But the big tree died; the Indian Trail Drive-In Theatre closed and is now a receptacle for wooden pallets, and the Indian Trail Nursing Home changed its name. So what would be the point?

A video
of Upper
Sandusky?

Gene Logsdon
June 17, 1992

Icould hardly believe my eyes when I read that Mayor Kenny Richardson of Upper Sandusky was ready to invest big bucks in a video of our fair town. Jeez. It's bad enough that everybody and their cousins are making videos of everything in sight. Stacks of videos grow on my desk, all from PR firms across the nation, all full of dreary little lies about how great their product or company is, all of them unviewed by me.

I tell the PR flaks not to send them, that if I give their new product a news spot at all in the magazines I write for, all I need is a modest little brochure that states a few pertinent facts. I do not have time to sit in front of a television set and watch these dumb videos all day. But alas, the videos are "in the budget" so they send them anyway.

Imagine how much greater is the output of videos from governmental offices where the officials can dip into tax money to pay for them. When they are not trying to start yet another festival or craft show, every town in the nation is making a video bragging about how much better it is than every other town.

The big things in life are the little things

Does the officialdom in any of these cases understand that nobody of decision-making power is going to look at these videos, much less believe all that malarkey? All expanding businesses are interested in is a pool of cheap, reliable labor and the size of the tax break small-town suckers will give them.

But if Upper wants to throw that kind of money around for a video, then I think the least it could do would be to hire homegrown talent. A few of us got together the other day and brainstormed the outline for a video of Upper Sandusky that at least would be fun to watch and not just another goody-two-shoes pack of lies.

Opening scene: A view from the courthouse tower, the camera sweeping over the town, focusing finally on the sun sinking behind U.S. Commission Company. Background music of Jimmy Dorsey's band playing his 1940s song, "Dusk Over Upper Sandusky."

A man is loading grain out of a corn storage building (grain is our principle commodity, get it?) and as the camera plays lovingly over this scene of rural integrity, the man drives away in his loaded truck. The camera follows him as he chugs out past Lite Star, turns around, rolls back into town, pulls into the front of the U.S. Commission, and sells the grain back to the company he has just taken it from. (The thief was eventually caught).

Segue to title in big yellow letters formed with ears of corn: "The town without a festival." Voice over (suggest using as narrator former Mayor Don Hall, who is unequalled in the art of expressing sarcasm in a soft, mellifluous voice): "This is the town that you will never forget; the town that will permit a home for unwed dogs within its boundaries, but not a home for unwed mothers; a town that wants a festival but can't find anything to be festive about; a town that even spells its name wrong, on purpose.

Camera zooms in to focus on a street sign that reads: South Sandusy Ave. Under the sign a woman is explaining to a reporter: "We spell it wrong deliberately, to attract the attention of the tourists."

Slowly the sign fades out of focus and zeroes in on typical street scenes: two drunks fighting in front of the Sandbox; pigeons dabbing the front of the bank with splotches of white; a lawyer preening in front of a store window; a motorist, cussing and pounding on a parking meter; a man running down the street toward the high school. Two vicious looking dogs are chasing him, fangs bared. The man stops occasionally to fend them off with his briefcase, upon which is written: Superintendent of Schools. He calls for help as he runs. Two senior citizens on a porch, polishing their golf clubs, watch in bored detachment.

"Think they'll get him?" the one asks.

"We should be so lucky," says the other.

Again the soft mellifluous voice. "This is a town of colorful contrasts, a season for your every mood."

The screen displays carolers singing Silent Night on the steps of the courthouse and just as the strains of "sleep in heavenly peace" fade beautifully away, the scene changes abruptly to an angry crowd of hunters and dog owners jamming into the courthouse and shouting threats against animal welfarists who have tried to tell them how dogs should be treated. Underneath the general uproar of protest can be clearly heard: "Let's run the sonsabitches outta town."

Scene changes to views of farmland. Voice over: "The land in and around Upper Sandusky is very fertile, producing, among other things, the tallest weeds in the world (flick to man standing in Reber's Bottom underneath 20-foot Giant Ragweed) and poison ivy that grows so verdantly that it sometimes passes for an ornamental. (Shot of my son and me cutting down huge poison ivy plant growing up the porch wall of the house he bought.)

Scene changes to a big tractor plowing through cattails. Narrator continues: "Upper Sandusky is proud of its innovative farmers. Here you see one of our finest, illegally plowing up wetlands in a drought year, so that when it floods the next year he can say he farmed it previously and maybe get government disaster payments."

A field of dandelions appears on the screen, the dandelion seeds blowing through the air like a blizzard. "Here is another example of innovative, efficient local farming. The government pays this farmer more money not to farm this field than he could make farming it, allowing him enough time to farm his other 4,000 acres and still have four-month vacations."

Closeup of farmer during four-month vacation, sitting in a bar, bitching because teachers get two-month vacations. Scene dissolves as camera focuses on butts bulging farther and farther out over the edges of bar seats.

Narrator: "But along with all these, ahem, examples of growth, Upper Sandusy, er, Upper Sandusky, stands for money growth, too. We boast more organizations for economic development per capita than any town of our size. Our ability to produce mission statements ranks second only to our ability to produce soybeans."

121

The big things in life are the little things

Segue to group of high schoolers doing dance routine on court-house lawn while rapping:

Thanks to R&E and CIC
Upper is the place to be.
Boards and bureaus grind their axes,
Scheme for funds from local taxes.
Come, bring money, our builders say,
So they can get rich, and move far away.

If the CIC & R&E are interested, I will rustle up a complete transcript along these lines and offer my services for something less than the price being quoted. This one comes with a money back guarantee to get attention.

The insane
mountains
of Harpster

Gene Logsdon
Nov. 12, 1986

If the first sign of insanity is to believe the world around you is going insane, then I'm ready for institutional care. Believing the world is mad has one benefit. If you are really convinced of it, you will never suffer a nervous breakdown because you realize that to worry about a world ruled by happenstance being acted upon by irrationality is itself irrational. The only proper response is to relax and giggle (like an idiot) until death do us part.

Case in point: the corn mountains in Harpster. If you haven't seen them yet, you are missing one of the great wonders of the world right here in Wyandot County. Pillsbury built the two mountains because there is no place else to put the corn and nobody wants it. The company could be making more money selling the mountains as tourist attractions than as corn, charging people to see them. Postcards would go well, and help publicity.

Of course the best time to see a corn mountain is when it is being built. Pillsbury has what I'm sure is the longest drag chain elevator in the world. To make a corn mountain, you crank that thing up till the snout is wreathed in cumulus clouds. Then you dump corn into the bottom of it, two truck loads at a time, and the golden grain whooshes up the elevator and tumbles out of the clouds onto the growing mountain. I kid you not, by comparison, the Grand Canyon is as boring as a child's coloring book.

One of the corn mountains holds 700,000 bushels. That is last year's excess corn. This year's mountain holds 900,000 bushels. What will next year's hold? By then the cornbelt grain handlers may vie for the tallest corn mountain, some with maybe two million bushels in them. I hope Pillsbury uses more imagination next year and shapes theirs into a ski slope. Why should we have to go to Michigan when we could ski right in Harpster?

The only reason Pillsbury or anyone else can afford to build corn mountains is that the government pays for it. In fact, there's more profit in storing corn this year than in growing it, and grain handlers have been seriously talking about filling a big limestone mine in southern Ohio with the stuff – literally dumping it down a hole in the ground. I don't know what the government is paying right now, but I think it's 27¢ a bushel per year.

That makes a corn mountain look like a fairly profitable enterprise even if the corn eventually rots away. But of course it takes a heap of money to make a corn mountain and then keep it covered with plastic and aerated. In comparison to the traditional grain elevator of yesterday, Pillsbury has a sizeable labor force and a huge payroll, so actually your tax money to pay for the corn mountains is funneling back to wage earners. This is another example of why the economy has not all gone to hell, as it should by any rational yardstick. The government, our biggest "business," takes our money in taxes but feeds most of it back into circulation, and the wage earners spend it. Thus we keep vigorous a mad merry-go-round of paper money.

Why not go a step farther? Why not, for a year, just pretend we are producing all this grain. Pretend we are planting. Pretend we are harvesting. Pretend we are hauling it to the elevator. Pretend to build mountains of it. Pretend to dry it. Pretend to dump it in holes in the ground. Pay the farmer what he'd make from the corn crop this year (nothing) plus his subsidy, on condition that he only pretends to farm rather than actually do it.

Look at all the natural resources we would save. All farm bureaucrats and agribusiness workers would get their paychecks as long as they only pretend to work. This would mean no change for a great many of them. Then all the cashless grain farmers could go fishing for a whole year instead of just half a year. Maybe we have reached the point where grain producers should just take every other year off. Makes a lot of sense in a mad world.

Could we have your radioactive waste, please?

Steve Zender
June 14, 1995; Aug. 20, 1997

I certainly hope Wyandot County seizes the moment now that folks are fighting over what to do with the waste from the Davis-Besse Nuclear Power Station.

As I have been saying for more than two years, if Wyandot County wants to be the King of Waste, we need the radioactive stuff.

We're already the dumping ground for the area's solid waste, but how exciting is that? Let's put some spice in our lives. Let's go for the big one. Let's go radioactive!

What could it hurt? We've already got a landfill, big hog farms, the possibility of egg "factories" with millions of chickens. All those things stink and none of them have the glamour – the glow, you might say – of radioactive waste.

Carey has its lime dust and the stench of pelletizing plants; Sycamore has its "world's biggest tire pile" and fights tire burning plant proposals; Lovell has pallet piles and smelly businesses, and Upper Sandusky is thick with lawyers. With all this already surrounding us, what harm could there be in a little radioactive dump?

And we're so close to Davis-Besse. We're a natural. If we can revive the proposed I-73 route and cut through our farmland, getting rid of all those wasted fields and stuff, we'll have even easier access to nuclear power plants throughout the country. Bring on the radioactivity!

Right now anti-nuke forces are out in full force because they don't want the government to allow Toledo Edison and other outfits like that to ship the radioactive waste to Nevada.

The newspaper reports haven't clarified it, but I'm assuming they mean Nevada, the state, and not Nevada, the town in Wyandot County. Because if it were Nevada, the town in Wyandot County, there would be little controversy. County government would have the welcome wagon warming up. "Take a dump in Wyandot County." That should be our motto.

As I understand it, the anti-nuclear people – the yellow-bellied wimps – don't want nuclear waste transported but they also have fought against using outdoor storage vaults. But now the anti-nuke people are saying, well, maybe it is okay to store it in sealed vaults. Just don't ship it around the country.

This is a nuclear-age conundrum.

Storing the Davis-Besse waste in Wyandot County would be a good compromise, don't you think? It's a short drive from the lake and we could store the waste inside. As you may recall from past columns, I propose storing the nuclear waste in the basement of the courthouse.

Isn't it about time for Governor Voinovich to visit Wyandot County again? Isn't there a road to open or a ribbon to be cut or something? Let's get the governor here so we can make a nuclear waste pitch!

As I've preached in the past, Wyandot County is a natural for nuclear storage because not many people live here. If something does go wrong, the number of people dead or dying with cancer will be limited to only 20-some thousand or so.

And what could possibly go wrong?

The state government has already convinced area officials that storing nuclear waste is a good, safe idea. They've even conducted seminars on the subject. Besides, if the government says it's so, it **must** be safe.

And even if a few people do get sick or die, think of the jobs it will create for those lucky enough to live.

Could we have your radioactive waste, please?

A few years back, Ohio started storing radioactive waste from nuclear power plants, hospitals and research labs for not only our own state but for Indiana, Iowa, Minnesota, Missouri and Wisconsin. (We must have won a lottery or something.) The other states will get their turn at storage some time in the future (probably after some sort of disaster befalls Ohio) so we need to get our share of the nuclear pie while we've got a chance. We need to takes steps to see that if Davis-Besse starts shipping its waste to Nevada, it's south to Nevada (the town) and not west to Nevada (the state).

If you're wondering why my first choice for the storage area for the radioactive material is in the basement of the Wyandot County Courthouse, it's so the Wyandot County Commissioners can keep an eye on it. Store the stuff there long enough and each one of them might be able to keep three or four eyes on it.

I originally suggested inviting Debbie Boone for a gala grand opening. But I'd like to alter that a bit. I think we should invite country music sensation Leann Rimes to sing her remake of the Boone classic, "You Light Up

Just plain old trash in Wyandot County. Nothing radioactive yet ... as far as we know.

My Life."

I realize the courthouse basement might be a little small to house all the radioactive waste from the entire country, so we might have to ask the commissioners to occasionally take some of it home with them. And maybe the governor could take a load back to his place after each visit to Wyandot County. We could also ask state representative Randy Weston to take some radioactivity down to his place in Morral and maybe state senator Karen Gillmor could take some to Old Fort, or Port Clinton or Dublin or wherever it is she lives. Cooperation, folks, that's what it takes to brighten Wyandot County's future.

The Other Ohio
and Wyandot
County's Little Five

Steve Zender
Oct. 7, 1994

Toledo better be careful. That town's leadership wants to decentralize state government so it can share in some of the political largess, but the plan might backfire.

The Toledo Blade says its city is located in the "Other Ohio." The Blade, Toledo government, and various other small cities in Ohio claim state government is only interested in Cleveland, Columbus and Cincinnati, at the expense of the other cities.

That might be true. Decentralization might be good. But let's not stop at the cities. What about us? What about Carey and Sycamore, Nevada and Harpster. What about Marseilles? (The one in Wyandot County, not France). We want to feed at the government trough too.

I figure that if Toledo gets some of Columbus' government action, the Little Five in Wyandot County might as well try to steal some governmental plums away from Upper Sandusky. And Toledo had better expect the little towns in Lucas County to steal government jobs from them. This might become a free-for-all.

The big things in life are the little things

The Blade editorializes that the state's resources are funneled to Columbus in particular. For the past five years the newspaper has urged more decentralization. "In this age of instant communications," says the Blade, "it is unnecessary to site the bulk of state government in the capital city. Why not, for example, locate the Department of Natural Resources in Toledo or Sandusky, on the shores of Ohio's greatest natural resource, Lake Erie? Why not put the Department of Agriculture in Bowling Green, in the heart of Ohio's richest farmland? Why not relocate the Bureau of Workers Compensation to Youngstown or Marietta, which would no doubt love to have such a substantial number of recession-proof jobs."

I can guarantee you that a great number of residents in Wyandot County's Little Five believe they are part of the "Other Wyandot County" located in the "Other Ohio."

Whether you agree with The Blade or not, they do make a couple of important points: most government jobs seem to be "recession proof," and having government offices in central locations are less important in this day of instant communication. So, if it's not as important to have your state government offices in the middle of the state, it stands to reason it's not as important to have your county offices all in the county seat. You could move the highway department to Carey; the health department to Nevada; the human services department to Sycamore; the sheriff's office to Harpster. The Blade suggests the Ohio Department of Natural Resources for Toledo or Sandusky, but I would suggest Marseilles (the one in Wyandot County, not France) because of Killdeer Plains.

Governor Voinovich disagrees with the "double standard" charge levelled against him and Nancy Hollister, the governor's running mate, told The Blade that, as a mayor, she was not ignored by state government. "It's a matter of getting your act together," she said.

So, there you go. Get your act together.

I'm assuming that "getting your act together," to a politician, means being prepared to lobby, gripe, plead, threaten, whine, yell and stomp your feet. You might also be forced to prostitute yourself in some way that makes you forever beholden to the state and/or federal government.

Always remember, decentralization can be a double-edged sword. Toledo might lose more jobs to little towns than it gains from Columbus.

There's one more thing to think about before starting to "get our act together." Are we sure we want all these bureaucrats moving in next door?

Battle of the burgs: Carey vs. Upper Sandusky

Gene Logsdon and Steve Zender
Ohio Magazine, September 1996

C arey and Upper Sandusky are about 10 miles apart, but they might as well be 10 hundred from each other, at least in the minds of some residents.

As historian George Knepper once observed, Ohio is less a state than a collection of feuding city-states. Cleveland trades insults with Columbus, Cincinnati contemplates secession, and Toledo wonders if it belongs to anyone. And when the dividing line is drawn in small-town Ohio, the name calling reaches the level of art form.

A native Upper Sanduskian (60 years) laughs as she relates an incident that "tells it all" in her opinion. "We took some friends who have lived in the Upper Sandusky area all their lives to see the famous Shrine of Our Lady of Consolation in Carey. It really is a remarkable church and worth seeing even if you don't believe in any religion. And it's one of the few churches in America to be named a Minor Basilica, whatever that is, by the Pope. Would you believe that our friends had never, ever visited the Shrine before? In their whole 50-some years of life. And as we were driving around

The big things in life are the little things

Carey, one of them said in surprise: 'Why, there're some pretty nice homes in this drinkwater burg.'"

The story does not surprise very many people who have lived here forever. Most Upper Sanduskians have never visited the Shrine. They especially avoid the Minor Basilica during the annual August pilgrimages. "That's when all those 'ethnics' come to Carey," explains a Scotch-Irish Upper Sanduskian, trying to be politically correct about Americans of Italian, Lebanese, Iraqi, Syrian, Greek and Chaldean descent who flock to the shrine from surroundings cities (especially Detroit – drat those Michiganders) every summer. Their emotional displays of faith embarrass those who favor the colder, Anglo-Saxon, northern European brand of Christianity.

Carey has been perceived as "Catholic" in Upper Sandusky, and Upper Sandusky as "Protestant" in Carey, and never the twain shall meet. A Protestant who lives in the countryside between the villages (he says he lives on the Maginot line) explains it this way, a faint smile on his face: "When I was growing up, my family displayed the typical Protestant view about the Shrine. We thought it was closely allied with the devil."

"Upper is the most bigoted town in the world," says a Carey resident. "For years Upper High kids would holler at us: 'Narrow streets, narrow minds,' referring to our main street, which they claimed was a foot or so narrower than Upper's."

"And the Carey teens would shout back: 'Broad streets, broad butts,'" says an Upper resident, smiling joyously at the recollection.

By the same illogical way that Carey is "Catholic" and Upper is "Protestant," Upper Sandusky is Republican and Carey is Democrat to the gray heads of the county. Doesn't matter that both Carey and Upper Sandusky, like most of the rest of rural Ohio, votes Republican. The two towns are convinced they're different and they're damn proud of it.

"Oh, for heaven's sake, don't get that silly thing started again," said Carey Village Administrator John Windau when we asked him how the two towns were getting along politically in recent years. "We've got our differences ironed out and we're getting along fine."

Meaning there used to be a problem?

"Well, Upper is the county seat, you know, and the largest village in the county. It has always seemed to the other villages that Upper took care of Upper first."

Wasn't that true?

The battle of the burgs: Carey vs. Upper Sandusky

"What's the use of getting into that now?"

A typical Carey gripe is that "Upper Sandusky forgets we're part of the county." A man in his 70s remembers working for a Carey firm doing plumbing work at the Wyandot County Courthouse years ago. "You'd think," he heard one courthouse staffer huff, "they could have found someone from Upper to do that work."

A year or so ago a group of Upper Sanduskians with noble intentions organized an effort to bring more industry to the county, but they seemed to be talking mostly about Upper Sandusky, not surrounding villages. Reminded of that, the new organization quickly broadened its focus and even invited Carey Mayor Dallas Risner to a meeting. He came, which surprised not a few people. But when the question of how the various villages ought to work together to bring in industry, a reporter wondered aloud how Carey and Upper could "cooperate" in landing a new business, since one town's gain would be the other's loss in property taxes and therefore school funding, a critical problem for both towns. (God forbid that the two towns might someday be in the same school district.)

A fairly long silence followed. When a member of the organizing group opined that what was good for Upper Sandusky would be good for the whole county, he unwittingly torpedoed the project's effectiveness, and it has floundered ever since. The mayor of Upper Sandusky refused to hire an administrator to oversee the program, as the group wished, and the mayor of Carey said he would have to "think the project over awhile." Since then the two towns have, typically, taken opposing positions. Upper's leadership has gone all out to drum up new business, while Carey declares it will encourage only quality business.

"Carey is just jealous that it can't get a Wendy's and a McDonald's like we've got," says an Upper Sanduskian, primly.

"Oh, sure," says a Careyite. "In this day and age, only Upper Sandusky would brag about having more chain stores and strip malls. Five years behind the times as usual over there. Before all that trash growth, Upper was almost as pretty as Carey."

In fact, "appearance" might be at the root of much of the rivalry, which is strong on the blue- vs. the white-collar theme. One telling observation: "When you try to picture Upper in your mind, you think of the dome of the courthouse under which a gaggle of lawyers and assorted other suits and ties are scurrying around, robbing the rest of the citizens. Think of Carey and what comes to mind is a dome of dust coming from National Lime and Stone

Company's stacks. Underneath are hard hats and blue collars, who are, of course, the types of people those guys in suits will be screwing."

Class consciousness fuels another gripe: "You go to a bar in Carey and you're considered to be an alcoholic or a hoodlum by the Upper Crust. But it's okay for lawyers, bureaucrats and other pillars of the community to hang out in bars in Upper or, better yet, up at Lake Erie watering holes where their neighbors can't see them."

Local conventional wisdom says Carey is far less classy and class conscious than Upper, but maybe that's because opportunity for upwardly mobile pride and prejudice has been lacking in Carey. "There is no hoity-toity social club in Carey like Upper's Elks," the locals will point out. Carey didn't even have a golf course (the game for the elite, right?) until the 1990s. Its name suggests a lack of interest in the social order: "Bob's Countryside."

The Upper Sandusky side of that story? Carey people lack tact. They're hicks.

An Upper Sandusky man who works in Carey describes the town's personalities like this: "If you're sitting in a restaurant and some guy you've had a disagreement with comes in, the Upper guy will wait until he leaves and say, 'I'm glad that son-of-a-bitch is gone.' A Carey guy will say, 'Hey, you son-of-a-bitch, come over here, I want to talk to you.'"

One favorite and totally true Carey story underlines its claim that Upper Sandusky really is afflicted with haughty hypocrisy. Carey found out that "Sandusky" was misspelled as "Sandusy" on the street sign at the center of Upper Sandusky. In great glee, The Progressor-Times, the Carey newspaper, published a photo of the street sign, with the courthouse looming behind it. An editorial accompanying the photo wondered, snottily, about the sanity of a town that wanted to lure in new business but couldn't even spell its own name correctly. When an elderly Upper Crustian was informed of the boo-boo by a Carey person, she stared for a few seconds, drew herself up as peerlessly as Hillary Clinton and replied: "We spelled it wrong on purpose, to attract attention."

One excuse for pretending vast difference in identity leads to another. If Carey is Democrat, then in the eyes of Upper it must be, bite our communal tongue, liberal. If Upper is Republican, then it follows in Carey that Upper is ultra-conservative. "Upper Sandusky is so conservative that the post office over there used to have a hard time selling stamps with Roosevelt's mug on them," says a Careyite. He no longer tells that story since discovering that in Upper Sandusky, it was being taken as a compliment.

Many think that sports, the true religion and politics of the country, are the main source of enmity, real and imagined, between the two towns. Upper and Carey high schools used to play each other annually in sports, and Upper regularly trounced the smaller Carey. Some say the schools quit playing each other because vandalism was getting out of hand. For years a rite of passage into manhood was to sneak into the opposing town with a paint brush and a can of paint and smear insults on any handy wall.

By the time the football competition ended in the '60s, the record was 36-14-6 in favor of Upper Sandusky. Upper says they won because their school was better. Carey says it was because Upper Sandusky's school is bigger. Upper says Carey quit playing them because it got tired of getting beat. Carey says Upper is lucky the series ended when it did because Carey's program has prospered, even including a state championship, while Upper's has floundered.

Now that the schools no longer play each other in football, the undercurrent of hostility seems to be subsiding so much that both towns claim their school children "hardly know the other town exists, and that's progress." But a few determined citizens still manage to keep the rivalry alive. A Carey resident who works in Marion alongside Upper Sandusky people, has shifted his focus to academics, which is like Ohio State suddenly deciding to go head to head against Michigan in medieval history. "I tell the Upper boys at work that we've got 'em beat every way," he says. "We're better athletically, academically and," he adds for good measure, "spiritually."

But after more than a half century of close observation and research into the mores of both towns, including a Ph.D. dissertation, it appears that the real reason the two villages have a difficult time kissing and making up is because of kissing and making out – sexual rivalry. In some cultures, raiding neighboring villages for mates was once a socially approved tradition, thus insuring healthy genetic hybridization. Upper Sandusky and Carey have been doing the same thing, but without much social approval or anthropological canonization. "Carey girls were fast," says an elderly Upper woman, recalling 30 or 40 years ago. "And so were the boys. My mother frowned on us dating them."

"Carey usually has prettier girls, I'll have to admit," says a young Upper man with a sigh, "but they also have the kind of guys who can keep them satisfied."

The big things in life are the little things

Love conquereth all. The Carey writer of this article is married to an Upper Sandusky girl (who, against much of the evidence, still insists there are very real differences between the villages.) The Upper Sandusky writer not only once lived in Carey (for a year) but argues with his numerous Carey relatives no more vehemently than with his numerous Upper Sandusky kinfolk. The generality that both writers will agree on with the least number of exceptions is that Carey is a beer and shot kind of place and Upper a mixed-drink crowd. In fact, Carey has a bar named "Beer and Shotz." It's owned by a Sycamore resident. Ah, Sycamore, Ohio, the third ranking village in Wyandot County. Now, there's another story.

Our ghosts
are ghostlier
than your ghosts

Gene Logsdon
Nov. 8, 1978

You might know. Carey has friendly ghosts but Upper Sandusky has an evil spirit. That's what our resident parapsychologist, Carol St. Francis, told The Progressor-Times, anyway. And I know of one person in Upper who might agree with her. Old Mrs. Beausay used to say there was an evil spirit lurking around the Busy Bee grocery, and she would walk out in the middle of South Sandusky Avenue when she passed the store to avoid it.

Neither Upper nor Carey need to feel smug about their respective ghosts. Dennis Barnes reports another possible ghost riding the country roads between Wyandot and Monnett. He swears he saw a mysterious horse and rider emerge from the morning fog out that way as he drove along a lonely road. The rider was dressed all in black with a black flowing cape – just like a character out of the 'Headless Horseman,' he describes it, appearing and then disappearing in a swirl of fog. I'm inclined to believe him even though he's not a parapsychologist, since the only weakness I've noted in him lately is a tendency to play a harmonica while waiting for traffic lights

137

to change, not a habit likely to lead to hallucination.

In fact, I'm inclined to believe Carol St. Francis and Mrs. Beausay too because when I was a kid there was always a ghost in the belfry of St. Peter's Church. If you think I'm kidding, just ask Edgar McCarthy or Don Brown or any of those other guys who led me astray in grade school days. Far be it from me to disagree with a parapsychologist, but I humbly submit that our ghost was not evil, but as friendly as any ghost Carey can produce. Or if not friendly, at least pious and God-fearing. After all, it lived in the church and it sure scared the hell out of me, which is something the good nuns could never do.

Everybody in school knew there was a ghost in the church bell tower. This sacred tradition was handed down from one generation of fifth graders to the next. One theory claimed a man had hung himself with the bell rope up in the tower (which tale, as I shall explain, was not totally false). Another theory said that bums slept up there someplace, an explanation that became popular after the picture show about Quasimodo (remember when we called them picture shows?). But whatever the rationalization, **somebody's** ghost groaned and moaned in the belfry and that was a fact so unquestioned that the door to the tower behind the organ in the choir loft never had to be locked to keep curious boys out. Until McCarthy, Brown and I came along.

I knew when we learned about the ghost in the fifth grade that we would eventually try to climb the tower, but it took us three years to work up enough courage. The first few attempts we only stood at the door to the tower and listened for moans. No moans in the sixth grade. None in the seventh. By eighth grade we knew it was now or never, since not even nuns are dumb enough to continue to believe we were going to church at noon recess to pray for the faithful departed.

D-Day finally arrived and armed with double-dares, giggles, and a flashlight, we stole up the choir loft steps in the dark, empty noon-day church and pushed open the door to the tower. Step by step we inched upwards in the cobwebby semi-darkness. Each step seemed an eternity of apprehension. Fear finally drove even our giggling to silence. McCarthy was above me, Brown below. All breathing heavily. I **hoped** it was us breathing anyway. Suddenly I felt a presence near at hand. A very heavy presence near at hand. It was, in fact, very heavy **on** my hand. "Ed, you're standing on my hand," I hollered. He had started back down the steps.

"Shut up," he said. "You hear what I hear?"

We heard. As sure as I'm sitting here writing this ridiculous story, we heard the most mournful moans and groans this side of hell.

Three very scared boys made Tony Dorsett look like a snail on our way to the street below. We told each other it was only the wind blowing through the organ pipes in the drafty tower, but we were in no hurry to go back and check out that explanation.

Those familiar with the peculiar bend of my mind can appreciate the dilemma I was now in. There were, make no mistake about it, groans and moans in the belfry, and I had no positive proof whether the wind or that ghost caused them. But if ghosts existed really, then logically enough it seemed, devils and angels and hell and heaven really existed too. If so, I had to change my way of thinking. I had always put ghost stories in the same category as the stories about there being a basement full of guns under St. Pete's and the stories about a tunnel between the rectory and the nun's house at the Carey Shrine, through which priests and nuns could move undetected to each other's living quarters. Just packs of lies. But now I wasn't so sure.

The ghost in the bell tower was no longer a matter of entertainment only, but the symbol of grave philosophical conclusions. I had to go back and prove or disprove its existence. Alone, as befitting great philosophical conclusions.

I got as far as the choir loft. Between the organ and the door to the tower I had to pass three short rows of pews. As I approached them, I saw a figure dressed in black lying as if asleep on the middle pew, with a white handkerchief over his (its?) face. It sat up, pulled away the white cloth, revealing the haggard, wizened, bearded face of an old man, staring at me quizzically. It did not disappear, but I sure did.

I'm as daft as a Leghorn hen, you think. Not so. There is an explanation for this seemingly ghostly experience. But it is not the kind of explanation to help the cause of priests and preachers who think the way to keep the faith strong is through fear. The old gentleman asleep in the choir loft was Jasper Lanker who, in his last years, became senile and was allowed the harmless habit of whiling away the hours in church.

No one ever hung himself with the bell rope at St. Pete's, but more authoritative folklore says a man did at Mud Church east of Upper.

And finally, though I've never found so much as a pea shooter in the basement of any Catholic church, there really was a tunnel dug between the priests' and nuns' house at the Carey Shrine. It was built to house steam, water and other pipe installations that served all the buildings from a central boiler and pump room, so I'm told by one of the Franciscans who used to be stationed at the shrine. He and I both surmise that when people saw the tunnel under construction, those who wanted to believe in the ghosts of old prejudices found evidence to support those beliefs.

And that's the moral of the story. There is a grain of truth in almost everything and out of it people believe what they want to believe. And someday I'm going in the bell tower and thank the ghost of old Jasper Lanker for teaching me that.

Spring migrants in welfareland

Gene Logsdon
May 25, 1983

The spring migration season is my favorite time of the year and this year it lasted longer than usual. On April 23, I saw my first yellow-rumped warbler up from the south, flitting among the oak trees looking for worms. Two days later, the first gray-crowned boater back from Florida hopped out of his van uptown, looking for the nearest senior citizen free lunch center.

Spring has truly come. And it was not until May 16 when I saw the last red-eyed mushroom hunter heading for Michigan, that I knew, sadly, the season was over.

But while it lasted we were enthralled by an unprecedented number of migrating birds and retirees – blackburnian warblers, indigo buntings, bald-pated golfers and even the secretive golden-age camper. But the biggest thrill of all was spotting a pair of rare tri-focal birdwatchers at Crane Creek, a gathering point of migratory species in Ohio, clucking excitedly at an even rarer white-eyed vireo.

The big things in life are the little things

The reason the migrants hung around a week or so longer than usual was the weather. Cold temperatures kept the foliage in the bud stage and insect activity at low ebb, and the birds had to linger, waiting for spring to catch up with them. For the migrating retirees, the reason for the delay was financial. Their problem was, and is, falling interest rates on CDs. They had to wait for dividends and Social Security checks to leaf out before they could continue to their northern vacation haunts in Canada.

Scientists are finding out amazing things about bird language, which they say has relevance for humans as well. Birds do not instinctively know their own birdsongs, as you might believe, but learn them from their parents, the way babies learn to communicate. The same species of bird has different dialects in different regions, believe it or not. A meadowlark in Ohio doesn't sound quite like a meadowlark in Minnesota. A cowbird, which lays eggs in other birds' nests, may grow up singing the song of the species in whose nest it hatched.

I wish National Science Foundation money were available to study changes in migratory retiree language, as well as for studying bird dialects. That might solve a growing mystery. Recent recordings of gray-crowned boaters, bald-pated golfers and hoary fishermen indicate quite a change in tune from what these migratory fellows sang before retirement.

Before retirement, you could plainly hear them say, chirping to the teenagers in their nests, that there was no such thing as a free lunch, and that the world didn't owe them a living. Now a change in their song seems to indicate that once past the age of 60, they think none of the moral philosophy applies any longer, and that the world does indeed owe them annual, 365-day vacations paid for by those nestlings to whom they preached that the world didn't owe them a living. Where did the migratory retirees learn that new song? Certainly not from their children. Certainly not from their parents either, who are rolling over in their graves, that their wealthy retired off-spring should grab every cent of Social Security welfare they can get their hands on while growing richer from the interest on the money they inherited.

Science believes the answer might lie in the Gold-Card Miser, a species of retiree who does not migrate at all, but, like the goldfinch, endures the northern winters quite handily. The Gold-Card Miser (invariably only the female of the species is sighted) is wealthy enough to finance two or three senior citizens centers and a Florida condo too, without denting his or her interest income. Yet happiness to a Gold-Card Miser is living on Social Security, half-free government housing, Medicaid, and senior citizen benefits, meanwhile banking more new money from dividends each year than was made at the height of his or her career.

The Gold-Card Miser is a solitary species sticking close to subsidized housing and rarely seen by anyone except the doctor. Neither male nor female speaks out on issues, fearing that the government would find a way to punish them by withdrawing all the welfare they don't need. They devote no time to community activities, being too busy saving money so the government will get most of it when they die.

One Gold-Card Miser, eating a free lunch at the Senior Citizen Center, was recorded as singing: "We need more government funds for our senior citizen activities." Asked why he didn't just spend a wee portion of his own small fortune, some of which he made in rather questionable schemes anyway, he chirped: "Why do you want to persecute the helpless old people like me? Look at the rich farmers. They're all on welfare. Why shouldn't we get our share of the gravy too?"

And so it has come to pass. A nation of buzzards.

Baby boom senior citizens

Steve Zender
Dec. 8, 1993; Aug. 16, 1995; July 2, 1997

I've been warning you for a couple of years now. The first of the baby boom generation started turning 50 last year and the rest of the world is going to have to contend with a bunch of grumpy, pushy old geezers who think they know everything.

I'm among the first baby boom wave so I can talk about this approaching problem from an insider's position. You people who are younger than the baby boom generation are going to hate us.

I hope I'm wrong. But I don't think so.

Ever notice how the people with more leisure time than anyone else are often the most petulant. They get the senior citizen discounts but they gripe the most and leave the lousiest tips. (Present readers are not included among these outrageous generalities, of course. All of our readers are kind, courteous, and extremely understanding. Did I mention generous?)

But, let's face it, many of those **other** people can be pretty irritating. Can you imagine what will happen now when the baby boomers retire? What a horrible thought. Can you imagine the children of the 1960s – those

144

pot smoking, free loving, irresponsible, protesting hippies – as senior citizens? And there will be millions of them. There were more of them to start with and, barring some plague, they'll be living (and griping) longer than any generation before. They will be brash. They will be demanding. They will be unmanageable. They will be irritating as hell.

If today's blue hairs are contemptuous, what will the baby boomers be like? They will be staging sit-down strikes at restaurants if their coffee is cold. Or too hot. Or the service too slow. Or too rushed.

There will be little old guys driving great big cars with golf clubs in the trunk and peace symbols on the doors. They'll be blocking six-lane highways and flipping off anyone who doesn't like it.

When they were kids, the baby boomers told each other not to trust adults. It's almost a certainty that as old timers, they'll be telling each other not to trust the young people.

They'll probably be especially ticked because politicians will be trying to cut their Social Security. And sooner or later the folks who offer senior citizen discounts are going to figure out that senior citizens have more money to spend than anybody. But forget trying to take bargains away from the baby boom seniors. They will be mad SOBs. And they'll let you know it. They've always spoken their minds and, because of their numbers, the people who sell things have pandered to them. They'll get their Social Security and their discounts, and then some.

The baby boom seniors will want the best tables; they won't want to stand in line; they'll want to save seats at crowded places; they'll want a discount; they'll be clamoring for a law making it illegal for whippersnappers under the age of 40 to drink; they'll be calling for a ruling that would not allow anyone under the age of 60 to serve in Congress. They'll want to go places faster, stay longer, pay less. They'll always want something made better and priced lower.

The world is going to cater to the boomers, not because they are better or smarter or nicer or more deserving. The world is going to pay attention to them because they have the numbers. Along with those numbers comes the time and money to buy things. And whenever one group has the money to buy things, another group will be selling something.

And if, for some reason, the baby boomers don't have the money? They'll burn their Social Security cards and their Depends and march on Washington until they get some!

The big things in life are the little things

Politicians don't like to face millions of angry old people who have bladder problems.

When you turn 50 you start getting pestered by organizations like AARP (Arrogant Army of Retired People) and receiving magazines "for mature adults." Right now these magazines are filled with advertisements for polka records and car cushions. Currently advertisers in these magazines want to sell you really comfy shoes that are white, pink or plaid with some sort of strap going over the front. They want you to buy ankle supports and pants with elastic waists.

This will change.

It will only be a matter of time before magazines like Secure Retirement will be featuring Elvis CDs and Rolling Stone retrospectives. Baby boomers, intent on staying young-looking into their mid to late 100s, will be into buying hair dye, face lifts and laser peels. Health food and exotic vacations will be the thing the old timers of the future will be buying.

I would guess the "senior citizen" magazines will still contain ads for sciatica relief, but my generation is not only going to **have** a pain in the lower back and buttocks, we're going to **be** a pain in that location.

I'll bet that before long you will begin hearing plenty of complaints over the very term "senior citizens." Too old fogyish for the baby boomers. Boomers just can't stop thinking of themselves as a bunch of carefree kids.

And then there is the sex thing.

Already the magazines for the "mature adults" are featuring full-page ads for items like the "patented penile support sleeve."

As Archie Bunker would have said, "Awww, geez, Edith."

It's only a matter of time before there is a congressional investigation into the questionable content of magazines for "mature adults."

"Senior" magazines will be shipped in plain brown wrappers to keep the contents from the eyes of impressionable 30-year-old sons and daughters.

Statistics show that religion also becomes more important as humans grow older. So the way I've got it figured, young people of tomorrow are going to have to contend with huge numbers of self-absorbed old people who are obsessed with their own well-being, appearance and sex, listen to a form of music other generations abhor, and think God is on their side.

Oooh, talk about a pain in the sciatica.

Bad news
for Upper
Sandusky

Gene Logsdon
July 26, 1978

The Bureau of Motor Vehicles has made a momentous announcement, one that will cause more consternation in Upper Sandusky than Nixon's resignation. According to Liz Bardon at the AAA office, the state says that in 1980, just two short years away, it is going to scrap our present auto tag numbering system.

On the face of it, that bit of news may not sound earthshaking, but in Upper it will cause social upheaval. You are prejudged in our town not by the length of your hair, mustache, pants or skirt, but by your auto tags. You don't really belong until you can acquire a three-digit U license, and all the people who really count know that the ultimate sign of success is a two-digit U license plate.

The only way to get one of these anymore is to inherit it or be the first one in the AAA office after the present owner dies. The license tag is Upper's substitution for a family coat of arms; it is part of one's identity and Upper natives take it a lot more seriously than the Bureau of Motor Vehicles would ever dream.

The big things in life are the little things

You know I'm not exaggerating, either. When I came back from college to good old Wyandot County, I couldn't figure out why people kept looking at me with such half-pitying stares. I noticed the looks most often when I was driving my beat-up, wheezing '51 Ford. So I traded for a newer model but the half-pitying looks only increased to whole-pitying looks. Only slowly did I realize the problem was my license tag, which was something like 1017649 T. There is nothing lower in Upper Sandusky, I learned, than owning tags with the letter T after the numbers – unless it was a set with WX instead of T. T indicates lack of social prestige perhaps, but WX is the pits.

Anyway, it took five years to work my way down to a T license I did not have to have a computer to remember – one with only four numbers which I can't remember. By then I was becoming acculturated back into the local society and craved for a U license like the other blue-bloods had. After all, my parents and their parents and their parents lived in this town. I was no fly-by-night newcomer and I needed my U license to prove it.

I demanded a U license. Easiest thing in the world to get: All you had to do was join the AAA. But all the AAA could do was get me a four-digit U number. In some ways, a four-digit U number loses you more face than a five-digit T number. With the latter, you can arrogantly display your independence from such stupid traditions, but a four-digit U shows you really **want** a "good" U license, but don't have enough pull or residence to get one.

Sigh. Heaven is to own 51 U, the lowest number you can get in Upper without paying extra. At least a dozen people are waiting around for the present owner of 51 U to shuffle off this mortal coil. There are true stories told around the AAA office of people who have actually come in, coveting a neighbor's nice, low U number, and suggesting that since the old geezer was not too well anymore, that his number be reserved for them. "Oh, you'd be surprised," says Liz at the AAA office. "It can really get ridiculous. I always tell people in divorce situations to get that license taken care of beforehand. You'd be amazed the fights that occur over who gets to keep the number."

I asked what I had to do to get the number 1 U, so I could one-up everyone. Liz says all I have to do is write to the proper office in Columbus, apply for the number, and if it isn't already taken, I can get it for $5 extra. If I want a tag that spells a name, like GENE, that will cost $45, if it isn't already taken. If the present owner of a desired number or letters dies, assuming there are several people waiting for the tag, you may have to know Governor Rhodes to get it. Or you can approach the present owner and offer him money. One Upper resident was offered $1,000 for his tag once, but he turned the offer down.

No other town in Ohio seems to attach such social importance to auto tags. In Carey, it seems, no similar custom prevails. Carey is more practical. As one resident (who couldn't remember her number when I asked) says, "I think some like to get lower numbers because they are easier to remember. I don't think there's any social importance attached to it."

Why the letter T is so unloved by old-time Upper residents is a mystery. It couldn't be, could it, because T is the identifying letter in Carey auto tags? Perish the thought.

Whatever, all the fun is going to come to an end in 1980. The state is going to take another status symbol away from us. Upper will never be the same. There will be no way to tell the good seed from the chaff. But at least I will not have to go through the rest of my life losing face with a four-digit U license.

Tanks for the miracles?

Steve Zender
Sept. 4, 1986

Y ou might know, cynic that I am, that the first thing I saw upon arrival was the man selling "I saw the miracle on the tank" T-shirts. And he was selling the shirt to a man on crutches.

Nearby were some people in a van, pointing flashlights at their "Image" photographs. "Three dollars?" one potential customer asked. "Don't you have any $2 pictures?" They didn't. Neither did the people selling photos a few feet down the road.

Yes, I paid a visit to Fostoria last week to see the image of Jesus and the child on the storage tank. Like most everyone else, I saw it. But a miracle? I think the biggest miracle involving the story so far is that no one has been killed in the traffic whizzing by on route 12.

We paid our visit at about 11:30 last Saturday evening and the place was filled with the curious. They were standing along the highway; darting to and fro across the road; gawking while driving by in their automobiles. I almost had a wreck before I got there, something about someone in the turning lane wanting to go straight and someone else in the straight lane wanting to turn. Avoiding that collision might have been the miracle of the night.

Now please, don't send the religious hate mail like you did when I defended rock and roll music. I don't listen to devil songs and I don't have one single thing against miracles. I just haven't figured out why the public is in such an uproar over oxidation on a tank that, with some imagination, resembles some folks' conception of Jesus. "Miracle on the tank" T-shirts? Come on. Our society is already shallow enough. Let's not totally cheapen it by making a religious experience out of rust.

I hope my skepticism about the image is not born of jealousy. After all, I'm from Carey, a home to miracles. Being loyal to my hometown, I wanted to shout last Saturday, "Hey, you want to see miracles and images, you should come to Carey! Haven't you heard about the rain that didn't fall on the procession from Frenchtown to Our Lady of Consolation? Haven't you seen the crutches? Thousands of people visit every year. Been doing it for more than 100 years." But I didn't say any of that stuff. I just kept my mouth shut and looked at the image across the highway. But I couldn't help but wonder: Will people actually begin making annual pilgrimages . . . to a tank?

You really can see it, you know. But a miracle? Why must this have some religious significance? Why can't people be contented to call it an unusual and interesting phenomena? Neat if you're a Christian; okay if you're a Muslim; irritating if you're an atheist.

I wish people would be a little more discriminating when they call something a miracle, else the world won't mean as much. When a parent calls the birth of a new baby a miracle, most of us will nod in agreement. But when Los Angeles manager Tommy Lasorda says God wanted the Dodgers to win the pennant in front of the home crowd, well, Tom, I think you're giving God a bad name. That's the way I feel about the image in Fostoria. I don't believe God is a Dodger fan. Neither can I imagine Him wearing an "I saw the miracle on the tank" T-shirt.

151

Let's put plum
pudding back in
Christmas, too

Gene Logsdon
Dec. 20, 1978

I haven't written my "Thoughtful-Thoughts-As-We-Enter-The-Christmas-Season" column yet, a prerogative we columnists insist on as steadfastly as preachers insist on their "Putting-Christ-Back-In-Christmas" sermon. Neither columns nor sermons make a tinker's dam of difference as to how the world lurches on, but tradition is tradition and far be it from me not to cooperate.

On Dec. 25, 42,000 B.C., Ottor the Hairy gathered his clansmen together in his cave to make a momentous announcement. After years of calculating, he had proven beyond the shadow of a doubt that day-length decreased from June 25 to Dec. 25 and then began to increase again. (He was only off three days which is pretty good considering he did not even have a pocket calculator to work with.) "This is the day the year turns on," he said. "This is the beginning of the new year. This is our promise from the Sun god that the warm days will come again. This is a day for celebration."

So the clansmen (any excuse will do) broke out their best food caches to eat and their best furs to wear and everybody had a ball in honor of the sun. By the year 41,980 B.C. the bash had grown to such excessive proportions that Ottor found himself warning his clansmen that they had become too extravagant, too materialistic. "You're spending far too much of our winter larder on this celebration. If you aren't careful, there won't be enough food left to see us through till Spring. It's the Sun we're supposed to be honoring, not our own gratification. Put the Sun back into Sun-Day and save your extra food and furs for the poor."

But the people did not listen. "We might as well eat, drink, and be merry," they said, "for tomorrow we'll probably be killed by sabertooth tigers." By 1,000 B.C., the celebration had outlived some 25 various gods of the sun and had assumed such gross and materialistic proportions in the Roman Empire that it took 12 days to do it up right, not to mention 30 days preparation beforehand and 30 days sobering up afterwards.

Pompous the Elder, leader of the Roman intelligentsia, spoke to Senator Flabbius who in turn spoke to the Emperor Corpulentia. Having the whole Roman Empire bombed out of its mind during the 12-day celebration of Saturnalia, he said, was causing a big loss in productivity along with a dangerous increase in spending, leading to a condition in the economy known technically as Inflationia. Flabbius and Corpulentia drew up a list of guidelines to restrict Saturnalian festivities for the people, but of course not for them, and Pompous the Elder wrote a canto on putting Saturn back into Saturnalia.

But by 200 A.D., the 12-day Saturnalia feast was bigger than ever. The Roman Empire was crumbling, just as Pompous the Elder had predicted, while the people engaged in shocking orgies. Even Christians, would you believe, attended the orgies, but only when they were out of town on business. "The only way to stop these sinful carnivals," preached Vesper the Good, "is to put Christ in Saturnalia and change the heathenish celebration into a day of prayer honoring the birth of Christ." Pope Sonorious III liked the idea and decreed that the new feast be called Christmas.

It didn't work out quite the way Vesper the Good had in mind. The people gathered to honor the birth of Christ all right, but then they went out on a 12-day binge, too. In fact, by the year 1574, Saturnalia was making a comeback throughout many parts of Europe and the clergy everywhere had to exhort the people to put Christ back into Christmas. To help the cause along, they put St. Nicholas into Christmas, too. In 1622 in England, Bishop

The big things in life are the little things

Geoffrey of Flannelmouth felt duty-bound to exhort the people to burn fewer yule logs so as to avert a fuel crisis. He also bemoaned the fact that people were starting to burn yule logs as early as Halloween.

The English did not give a damn about Bishop Geoffrey or his fuel crisis. They grew their hair longer and continued partying in, so it was said, the most scandalous fashion. In reaction, the Puritans arose. Puritans kept their logs in the woodshed, awaiting the final doom. Puritans always looked blue in cold weather as a result. Their laws were called Blue Laws. The number one Blue Law was the elimination of Christmas celebrations.

Now you know why the Puritans were run out of England. Over here Puritans found Massachusetts much colder than Merrie Olde England, so it was not long before people began putting yule logs and rum back into Christmas. St. Nicholas had been taken out of Christmas but by 1782, he was back.

But it was not until 1958 A.D. that Americans gave much thought to putting Christ back into Christmas – along about the time, coincidentally enough, when Hallmark decided to put special emphasis on a new line of religious greeting cards. In 1969, in the best traditions of Bishop Geoffrey of Flannelmouth, Vesper the Good, and Pompous the Elder, Gertrude Nosegay of suburban Chicago launched a campaign to persuade people not to cut evergreens for decorations, lest we run out of trees.

My fond wish for all of us this Christmas, 1978, is that soon, very soon, somebody will put roast goose and plum pudding back into Christmas, too.

Spring tune-up with the Old Softball Nut

Gene Logsdon
April 8, 1987

L ast Sunday I went out into a field to pick up a softball I'd hit and found an Indian tomahawk instead. Now tell me, where but in Wyandot County could that happen? We live in the most exciting place in the world. But don't tell anyone or we'll be swarming with tourists.

The softball (if not the tomahawk) reminded me that I had not seen the Old Softball Nut all winter. Where softball players go in cold weather is a mystery. Right after Labor Day they evaporate only to appear like flies as soon as the weather warms up, practicing their spits and limbering up their cuss words. I went down to the park and sure enough there was OSN, watching some youngsters playing ball.

"Watch that kid on second base," he said, without looking up. "He's the nastiest little scrapper out there. Knocked down the second baseman. Argues every play. Disgusting little snot. When he grows up a little I want him on my team."

"OSN, where do softball players go all winter?"

"Coonhuntin'. They'd rather hang out in the woods than party or go to Florida or any of that crap. They spend their money on coondogs and then spend all night trying to find where the damn things ran off to."

"Is it fun?"

"Nuthin' like it. Stumbling in the dark, getting torn up in blackberry brambles, falling into cricks. Almost as much fun as belly-slidin' in the dirt. Keeps you in shape. Nobody can walk like a good coonhunter. You take Jim Overbee. He can walk faster after a coondog than he can run under a fly ball."

I asked him how the softball season was shaping up for 1987.

"Hard to say. Last I heard, they were going to have eight divisions, two teams to a division. Then no matter how bad Commercial Bank is, they can't come in any worse than second."

"Come on now. There's only going to be three divisions."

"Yeah. Us and Bowen's and Bookies will be in one and the rest in the other two. So our record will be 0-26 even though we can beat all the other teams in town. That's democracy in action."

"I heard you were retiring."

"Yep, I've done it 11 years in a row now, so I expect I can do it again."

"Who's going to take the league, really."

"The team that wins the most games, unless it's us and then they won't count all the games."

"Be serious."

"Well, probably us, because we've got this new strategy. In the qualifying round, we're going to lose half our games. Then the rest of the year we'll only have to play wimpy teams like Commercial Bank and Schmidt Machine."

"You win by losing. Sounds like a good concept for modern life."

"Hey, dumb writer, don't you get holier-than-thou with me, or I'll nail you on your anti-tax writing."

"What do you mean by that?"

"You play a lot of softball, doncha? Why do you think it is such a popular sport?"

"It appeals to everybody."

"Yeah. Especially to sponsors. You can take a business deduction for sponsoring a team. We're all out here havin' fun partly at taxpayer expense. You don't think all these teams could have all these fancy uniforms otherwise, do you?"

And then he hooted. "The whole advertising world is built on tax dodges, dumb writer. You wouldn't have a magazine or a newspaper to write for otherwise."

A proliferation
of towels

Gene Logsdon
July 9, 1997

I know the growing overpopulation of bathroom towels is a man problem, not a woman problem, but I don't know if it is a man problem just in our family or in everyone's family. Maybe you can help me. I only frequent three bathrooms: ours, my daughter's, and my sister-in-law's in Kentucky.

It started several years ago when we were visiting at sister-in-law's home. There were three towels and accompanying washrags hanging at the ready in the bathroom. Since there were guests staying overnight I did not at first think that was unusual.

I selected the rose-colored towel and washcloth with lavender silk flowers embroidered around the border even though, well, the embroidery did not make a very practical surface for scrubbing behind my ears and toweling off my back. When in Rome, etc. My wife happened to barge into the bathroom about that time, and the look she gave me would have withered poison ivy.

"You're not supposed to use **that** towel," she said.

A proliferation of towels

How was I to know my towel was the yellow one with the lace border? Or the pink one with the lattices of blue ribbon bows sewn all over it? She ripped open a drawer and shoved a more conventional towel in my face. The thing I was mangling was a decorative work of art, not a real towel, stupid.

As you might imagine, it was not long before towels began to take over our bathroom at home, too – exquisite towels from many nations, to be admired but never touched. The first time such elegance appeared on the hanger above the tub, I was not sure.

The difference between towels-for-using and towels-for-looking-at was diminishing rapidly. "Wow," I said loudly. "What pretty towels." Quick footsteps approached from the kitchen and Wife snatched the towels off the hanger with one hand and replaced them with normal towels with the other.

Since you learn that wives can be asked how, what, or where, but never why, I did not ask about this strange behavior. I figured it out. We had company most of the day and Wife wanted company to see elegant towels when they went to the bathroom. Unlike me, everyone else in the world evidently could tell the difference between towels to use and towels to look at.

The towel business must be very good these days. Why didn't I buy stock in Cannon 10 years ago?

At my daughter's home, where I love to go because I get a king's treatment, everything is beautiful and always in order. I counted 11 towels and washcloths of various sizes on display in the bathroom reserved for us: two sets of washcloths, hand towels and bath towels, one for each of us; two sets of decorative washcloths and towels; and, mysteriously, a towel folded on the sink. "What's that towel for?" I asked my wife. "For wiping off the sink, which you never do, after you are done slopping all over." Oh.

Soon enough, a folded towel appeared on the sink at home too, and now there is another one, on the edge of the bathtub. I presume that is for wiping up water I slop on the edge when taking a bath. But I'm not about to ask why.

After the big blizzard, an epidemic of insecurity

Gene Logsdon
Oct. 25, 1978

T he people of Wyandot County have been acting stranger than usual, which is pretty darn strange anyway.

What would a psychologist say, for instance, about a fellow who buys a woodstove, a piano and a plane ticket to Hawaii, all on the same day – and who has a xylophone in his mouth where most of us have teeth? You might say that such things happen to editors who write too many newspaper columns, but that's not it. Not at all.

What's happened is that a serious outbreak of infectious Viral Insecurity has hit our fair county, and it's affecting us all. I know because I went out and bought two stoves (one cannot let one's editor one-up one, can one?). Now I have two fireplaces, a woodstove, a gas stove, an electric stove and a pantry full of red peppers in case none of them work.

But at least it's not we newspaperers who are starting all these false rumors about the weather. We've always left that to the weathermen. Ever since the kids went back to school in August (only extremely insecure school officials would make kids go to school in August), they kept bringing home rumors about a terrible snowstorm that was supposed to hit on Oct. 13. This stupidity was repeated, enlarged upon, refined until we knew exactly what time of day it would arrive (early morning), how it would attack (slush, turning to driving powder to six-feet deep) and how it would end (abruptly and melt in two days). Was it merely school children wishfully dreaming, wanting to get even with authorities who made them swelter in August classrooms?

I would think so, except that this kind of weathermongering has been going on ever since we almost froze to death last January. Every 10 days thereafter until the middle of April, I heard at least one rumor of another terrible impending snowstorm. None occurred.

Through the summer the weathermen nurtured our fears with predictions of terrible impending snowstorms this winter. And though a few voices of scientific sanity keep reminding us that the odds against another winter like last are over 100 to one, we prefer to believe the worst and go on buying woodstoves. There is not enough seasoned wood in the county to feed half of them.

To cover my insanity, I tell everybody that I'm a stove collector. I'm investing in stoves the way some people invest in gold (another symptom of Infectious Viral Insecurity). When trading in woodstoves hits it peak in December, I'll sell out and double my money. Better than pork bellies or sugar.

Your standard, run-of-the-mill psychologist says that insecurity is the first stage of manic depression – the first sign of a mind slipping into the looney bin. But as usual, the psychologists have it backward. Only an idiot can feel secure in the world we live in today. I'm trying to catch up on world news in the stack of Time magazines mounting on my desk – I'm only up to last July and already I'm scared witless about what is going to happen to us last September.

Show me something to feel secure about. Why, rumors floating around say there was something suspicious about the Pope's recent death. When a Pope can't even die in honorable peace, what chance do the rest of us have? Probably the CIA infiltrated the Sistine Choir and learned that John Paul was not really John Paul at all, but a Soviet spy just about to excommunicate the College of Cardinals. This would worry everyone, even the Arabs, and when the Arabs feel an attack of insecurity coming on, they raise the price of oil again.

The big things in life are the little things

No sir, only a fool can feel safe anymore. Even Woody Hayes, Ohio's own Pope, is no longer secure. He never was, to tell the truth. Woody never learned how to pronounce the word "pass." When ever he tries to say it, it keeps coming out "p-p-p-p-run" There's nothing wrong with Woody's ability to talk, God knows. But only secure people like to throw forward passes.

Woody proves my point: insecurity is a virtue. Look how long he has held his job, playing it safe. I bet he has a basement full of stoves, too.

Not that the stoves will heal a case of insecurity. If I light a fire in my woodstove, I'll probably burn the house down. If I turn on the gas stove, the gas will probably leak and blow the house up. If I stick with electric heat, I will have to sell the house to pay for it. Might as well dig a hole in a snow-drift and hibernate with a wool blanket and a bushel of hot peppers. Just my luck a warm spell would come along sudden-like, melt the snow and drown me in my sleep.

Man's best friends?

Steve Zender
*Nov. 30, 1994, and selected
columns prior to 1983*

T he only way to start a fight faster than talking about religion, politics or sports is to say something bad about a person's pet. You can criticize a kid quicker than a pet. Say "I hate cats" and you are going to get in trouble with a segment of society.

Well, I don't exactly hate cats (although I did give Roger and Judy Jenot the book "100 things to do with a dead cat"), but pets in the Zender household tend to cause problems.

My wife and kids dearly want a cocker spaniel for a pet (and I sort of do too, I sheepishly admit) but I know that any pet that steps paw into our house will do things to drive me absolutely nuts.

Take Jasper, for example. Jasper, the cute, cuddly little yellow cat that would attack a newspaper – while you were reading it. He was the cat who wanted to claw anyone with red hair (nephew Tom will attest). You've heard of "climbing the walls?" Jasper would try it. He enjoyed riding around (and around and around) on the stereo turntable. He was the cat who was finally exiled to a friend's farm after he (the cat, not the friend) decided to spray the baby's new, frilly bassinet prior to the baby's arrival.

Before the cat left he had managed to wreck most of the house. He climbed curtains and did a million other dastardly deeds, including tipping over a full box of soap powder. Well, actually, I knocked over the soap, but I was chasing the stupid cat, so it was his fault. Jasper even indirectly damaged the clothes dryer. That's such a long story I'm not even going into it but if you read on I will tell you how the goldfish caused $100 worth of damage to the dishwasher.

So far we haven't bought a dog because we know it would probably end up flattened on main street. And birds are out. My wife hates birds, probably something to do with all those years of feeding chickens on the farm.

The hermit crabs froze in the blizzard of 1978.

Then came the hamsters. Despite bearing a decided resemblance to rats, the hamsters were loved by our kids. I guess they got a kick out of hearing their grandmothers scream at the sight of them (the hamsters, not the kids). Anyway, hamsters, as all owners of hamsters already know, have a tendency to escape from their cages. Naturally, ours did.

Our hamsters didn't want to go behind the refrigerator or the couch or under the TV set. They went to the furnace.

They were in the cold air pipes of the furnace for hours until finally, in the wee hours of the morning, both were captured and returned to their cages, beady little eyes peering from behind layers of dirt.

Our house has one of those inefficient coal furnaces which was converted to gas. And left in the wake of the capture were various pieces of the cold air ducts which wouldn't fit back together like they once did.

Fish seem to do well in our house. At least they have not, as yet, escaped.

I should say some fish did okay. There was Swimmer, the killer goldfish who was constantly on the move, like a shark, and would chase all the other fish in the bowl until he killed them. Swimmer lived for such a long time that we watched him grow bigger and bigger. I came to the conclusion that one day he would grow so huge that he would shatter his bowl and demand residency in the bathtub.

Swimmer finally passed away and our house was serenely petless for several months. Then came the Wyandot County Fair last September and the two girls brought home a goldfish apiece. Throw a ping-pong ball in the bowl and you get the fish, the bowl and the water. Just a dollar apiece. Such a deal. Our third daughter wasn't born yet or we would probably have three fish.

Anyway, the fish are still alive. But they came close to death a few weeks ago and that was when they caused $100 worth of damage to the dishwasher.

The fish were on the kitchen counter, directly above the dishwasher, because they had been moved from one of the other rooms when the Christmas decorations were being put up. The fish were minding their own business when Sue (the bird hater) accidentally hit the fish bowl with another bowl. It was a light tap, but it was good enough to break a hole in the bottom of the fish bowl. Water gushed out of the bowl, along with things like the fish's "home sweet home" sign, the plastic grass and the stones at the bottom of the bowl. For some reason, fish demand stones and plastic things in the bottom of their bowl.

The fish swam for dear life, around and around (sort of like Jasper on the turntable), and escaped from being whisked out of the bowl by the gushing stream.

The water was sopped up and the stones picked up. Or so we thought. Just our luck, the door of the dishwasher was slightly ajar. Stones fell in and trinkled down to the inner works of the machine (even faster than Ronald Reagan and David Stockman had suggested). The first time the dishwasher was used, there was a grinding sound. A $100 repair bill followed.

Epilogue: Following being banished to the farm following the infamous bassinet spraying, Jasper, during a severe winter, "bought the farm" on which he was living. Cat of Satan was dead. The Zender family managed to avoid being talked into buying rabbits and a goat but did eventually purchase a cocker spaniel. (See "Maggie was a good old dog.")

Williams'
Circle

Steve Zender
May 16, 1990, and
Ohio Magazine, November 1994

I t was those damned cigarettes that caused the problem. If you don't believe me, ask Charlie Buckland, one of Fred Williams' friends and co-workers at the post office. (Or at least he used to be his friend.) Charlie and I gave up that nasty smoking habit years ago but Fred just won't do it. Despite the insults and the name calling, Fred still drags on those awful things. He just had to stop at O'Flaherty's Marathon for his pack of smokes. That's when the trouble began.

When our hero pulled into the downtown Carey service station he was apparently having a nicotine attack. He leaped from his car, leaving the door open, and the engine idling rapidly.

As he started to enter the building, his unoccupied car, a blue 1981 Dodge (it's the one that now has the passenger's side sort of smashed in), backed out of the station toward Vance Street. The car went over the curb. It was backing toward Houk Hardware, but the front wheels were turned just right as the car hit the street, so it made a neat little counterclockwise move and headed back toward the Marathon station. Missing the gas station, the

166

car completed its orbit and headed back toward the street again.

Fred, seeing all this, was obviously concerned. He wondered aloud if he shouldn't try to jump in the car and shut it off. But, geesh, it was going so fast.

John O'Flaherty, the station's operator, is not one to get excited. He told Fred to stay away from the car. Someone could get killed trying to stop that thing. "Besides," he said calmly, "It'll eventually hit something and stop."

Randy Smalley watched the first portion of this drama while stopped at the traffic light, but he pulled into the station to get a closer look. Where's a video camera when you want one, he wondered, as the car went round and round. He was relatively certain he could have won the $10,000 prize for the best effort of the week on the "Funniest Home Videos" TV show.

Randy pulled into the parking lot, a safe distance from Fred's runaway car, and then began wondering if that had been a smart thing to do. "John, would those gas pumps blow if the car hits them?" he asked.

"Nah ... I don't think so."

"John, could maybe those wheels get turned just so and the car come through this big window?"

"Nah ... I don't think so."

The car kept circling. John still had no doubt that it would eventually stop because it kept hitting that utility pole out by the street a little harder each time it went by.

All the details are not clear, but John reportedly made two phone calls while Fred's auto was making its laps. Fred, anxiously watching his car, wanted John to call the police and he didn't notice the significance of one question John asked: "What's the number of the post office?" Fred gave him the answer: 396-6664. One call went there, to alert postal employees of the event. The next was to the cops. "Let's see," John asked. "Should I dial 911? Is this an emergency?"

"Hell yes, it's an emergency," Fred barked.

The police, just down the block, arrived in seconds after the call, just in time to see the car mercifully smash into the pole and stop long enough for Fred to reach inside and turn off the key. Police officer Donnie Myers later lamented the fact that he wasn't at the scene. "I'd have shot out the tires," he laughed.

The big things in life are the little things

Nobody knows how many laps Fred's car completed, but guesses are at least 20, enough to provide amusement for the postal workers who had come outside to see the show, and for early morning travelers along Findlay Street.

I was at the post office Monday morning and during the short while I was there, several "well-wishers" stopped by to discuss the incident with Fred, proving once again the loving and caring nature of people who live in a small town. I suggested to Fred that it might be wise to take the next week off to avoid them.

Many people expressed similar condolences to Fred not long ago when the same car decided to put itself in reverse, smash into his garage, and knock the building off its foundation.

On the brighter side, there is now a sign at the site of the latest crash. Seems the area is now known as "Williams' Circle."

Yes, Virginia, there really are Yuccies

Steve Zender
From 1984 to the present

L et us hark back to how it all began.

In the beginning, 1984, a magazine named Newsweek declared that 1984 was the Year of the Yuppie.

This made me angry.

There is nothing intrinsically wrong with a Young, Urban Professional (Yuppie). But what a slap in the face to those of us out here in the country for Newsweek to name the entire year after them.

In 1984 America was in love with its president for a change, and that might have been nice, but he was the ultimate Yuppie, with the exception that he was old. The country had a money and power fixation. Too many young men were dreaming of being another Donald Trump. Too many guys wanted to wear suspenders. (Hey, didn't suspenders belong down on the farm?) Too many people were chasing martinis with Maalox, playing, yech, tennis, and driving fancy foreign cars with cellular phones in them.

The big things in life are the little things

"Give me a break," I said. "I know people with cellular phones in their combines. What about us? What about the good, hard-working decent folks out here in the country?"

What could I do about this Year of the Yuppie stuff, I wondered. And then I remembered that I owned a newspaper. If Newsweek could name a year after a group of people, so could I. So, as publisher of The Progressor-Times and The Mohawk Leader, I announced that 1985 was the Year of the Yuccie, the Young, Unhurried Country Citizen.

The national media ignored this announcement.

So did the vast majority of our readers.

But I didn't mind because I figured it would take time for people to understand Yuccism, even those who already were Yuccies but didn't know it yet.

And I was right. Well, sort of. Yuccie awareness has grown. After talking about the official Yuccie T-shirt for years, I finally had some printed. Up until that time I told fellow Yuccies we had just one T-shirt and they would have to wait their turn to wear it. The first Yuccie members, Yuccie Bob in Risingsun, Yuccie Marilyn in Upper Sandusky, and Yuccie Tim out there in California, seemed to understand but I think they suspected the truth: there was no official Yuccie shirt.

But there is now and all three original members were given free shirts for their patience. Yuccie Brewster, the official mascot, is pictured on the front of the shirt, hoisting his beer (or is that rootbeer?) and the official Yuccie logo is on the back. If I wasn't too old to say "cool," I'd say they are really cool.

The folks here at Yuccie World Headquarters designed membership cards and I laminate them with my own two hands. We have even made some country singers, including Vince Gill, Joe Diffee, Charlie Daniels and Patty Loveless, honorary Yuccies. I'll bet they were really impressed.

But in case understanding Yuccies hasn't been high on your priority list, maybe some explanation is in order.

First off, Yuccies don't really have to be young. If I'm going to start an organization, I don't want to get drummed out of it because of my age.

The most important thing to remember is that Yuccies are to the country what Yuppies are to the cities. If you are from a town that reminds you of Mayberry – and you're damn proud of it – then you are well on your way to understanding what Yuccies are all about.

When Yuccies think, they think "relaxed and happy." When Yuccies think of Yuppies they think ulcers and traffic jams.

You don't need to have anything against Yuppies, you just need to think the Yuccie way of life is better. More sensible. More livable. Honest.

Yuccies can live anywhere, but the really heart-and-soul Yuccies live in, or came from, places like Carey, Ohio, where a really nice library sits right next to the town's grain elevator.

A Yuccie town probably isn't going to make the top 10 list of the best towns in America and that is because the people doing the naming won't be Yuccies. But most Yuccies don't care much about lists so they won't know or care about the ranking.

Yuccies loved flannel shirts long before alternative rock groups started wearing the things. And, whether they have a phone in their combine or not, there is something about seeing someone talk on a phone while driving a BMW that really pisses off an honest-to-goodness Yuccie.

There is no official Yuccie music, though country would obviously be at the top. You can be a Yuccie and love opera, but you might be looked upon with suspicion. A "don't ask, don't tell" philosophy is suggested.

Yuccies have eaten Wheaties for breakfast. They love their country but gripe about politicians, maybe even more than most people, possibly because there are few – maybe no – Yuccie lobbyists.

Your typical Yuccie will love sports but there is a good chance there will be hatred for athletic teams from either coast. A Yuccie very likely bowls or has bowled in a league. Yuccies might golf but very few play at country clubs, which seems a contradiction in terms, doesn't it?

The fanciest bar in a Yuccie town might be the American Legion, VFW or Eagles. And in the best Yuccie communities, if you've spent too much time in any of those places, a policeman a lot like Andy Taylor would probably rather drive you home than arrest you.

Andy Taylor should be the role model for Yuccies: unpretentious; unsophisticated, yet wise; a little ornery; a tender streak but tough when he needs to be.

Andy is blue collar. He has an open mind but is a little stubborn. He can be independent but he understands the value of cooperation and preaches that philosophy. He is kind, but damn it, Barney, now you better not push him too far or you're going to make him mad.

The big things in life are the little things

A Yuccie community leader would like his town to "better itself," but realizes that "bettering itself" is a subjective idea. A good Yuccie town doesn't delude itself by trying to be something it's not. Good Yuccies wouldn't picture Mayberry as perfect, but would be darn proud to have a town just like that.

Residents of Yuccie places appreciate the good things they have: safety, friendship, and a sense of belonging that comes with living in a small place. Residents of a Yuccie town might be independent and outspoken, yet will come running when some person or some project needs help. A Yuccie town is like a family that squabbles among itself, yet circles the wagons when attacked from the outside.

Real Yuccies might not own a pick-up truck, but they've at least ridden in them from time to time. The police chief probably owns one.

Yuccies don't have anything against making money but they like the fact that it is probably very difficult to tell a rich Yuccie from a poor one. You remember some time back when the stock market took a tumble because the unemployment figures had dropped? The Yuppies were bailing out of the market because too many people were working! Meanwhile, the Yuccies, because they were working, were buying that new fishing gear down at the mall from the companies whose stock had plummeted because all those Yuccies had jobs.

Yuccie Brewster

Confusing, isn't it?

By the way, we do have an honorary Yuccie working for the Wall Street Journal, that bastion of the Yuppies. Clare Ansberry wrote up Carey in the Wall Street Journal in 1995. I told her it was obvious she understood

Yuccie things. During the course of several hours of interviews, she once asked about the Yuccies. "Let me get this right," she said. "It's a joke, but it's really not a joke."

Yeah, that about sums it up.

Real Yuccies wonder about Yuppies who want to "bring small-town charm" to blighted cities. Yuccies are small-town people who already live in the "charm" every day. And, strange as it sounds, there are people in those wonderful Yuccie places who are constantly trying to turn their charming little village into one of the blighted cities from which others are trying to escape.

Yuccies who live on the farm or in small communities realize their little place isn't, by standard measure, a center of culture. But they figure if they need or want culture, they know how to get there. And the Yuccies who don't live in little places at the very least understand what a great life that can be.

I once answered a guy who asked, "What the hell is a Yuccie?" by saying, "It's a person who would rather take the chance of being injured in a pick-up truck-manure spreader collision on a country road than being killed in a drive-by shooting on a crowded city street."

Yuccies aren't really looking for a fight, but they're a self-confident lot overall. There is really no need for Yuccies and Yuppies to be adversaries. But, for the sake of argument, if the two groups ever come to blows, bet on the Yuccie town. Any good Yuccie knows, "my town could whip your town."

photos and artwork

Book design by Mary Kromer and Steve Zender.
Cover art by Jenny Barnes.
Photos of authors by Sue Zender and Amy Zender.
Photos on pages 2, 47, 71, 104, 118 and 127 by Dennis Barnes.
Photo on page 13 by Steve Zender.
Photo on page 17 by Gene Logsdon.
Photos on pages 20 and 107 by Sue Zender.
Photo on page 90 by Toni Ahlberg.
Artwork on page 172 by Pete Fox.
Those who provided photos: Ann Mangett, page 7; Robert Hayman, page 55; D.C. Dannenhauer, page 71; Gertrude Stubbs, page 73; Sue Zender, page 78; Patty Bardon, page 86; Sara Nye, page 90; Jocelyn McClain, page 101, Steve Zender, page 110.

composition

Composition and design work for this book was done at the office of The Progressor-Times in Carey, Ohio. Text is set in Times, with headlines in Palatino italics. Bylines, dates and page headings are set in Helvetica, bold and bold italics. Software used was QuarkXPress. Photos were scanned, then "posterized," using Quark software.

Printing was done on 60-pound Lakewood white paper by BookCrafters, Chelsea, Mich.

Gene Logsdon, the well-known author of more than a dozen books, writes regularly for Ohio Magazine and has written for Organic Gardening, New Farm and various other magazines throughout the country. His "Country Rover" writings have earned him the title of the state's best columnist at the yearly Ohio Newspaper Show for weeklies.

He grew up on a farm in the 1930s and is best known for his essays, books and columns on rural society and the need for agricultural reform. Three of his most recent books are "The Contrary Farmer," "At Nature's Pace," and "The Contrary Farmer's Invitation to Gardening."

Proud of his reputation as a curmudgeon, Logsdon has provided wit and wisdom which has both amused and outraged Progressor-Times readers for more than 25 years.

Logsdon lives in rural Upper Sandusky, just down the road from his boyhood home, where he writes, tends to a few animals and raises fruits, grains and vegetables. He and his wife Carol have two grown children.

Steve Zender has been a weekly newspaper publisher since 1968. During most of those years he has written his opinions in a column called "Small-Town Boy," dispensing praise and criticism and, in general, having fun with small-town life.

Zender started his own newspaper in his home town of Carey, Ohio, while still a 21-year-old college student, eventually purchasing The Carey Times, a newspaper that has been published continuously since 1873. The Mohawk Leader, a 104-year-old Sycamore, Ohio, weekly, later became a sister publication.

He has been named the state's best columnist for weeklies in the annual Ohio Newspaper Association competition. Writing for Ohio Magazine, he also received first place in human interest reporting in the Press Club of Cleveland's Excellence in Journalism awards.

The Progressor-Times has received numerous state newspaper awards throughout the years in news coverage, advertising, design and other categories. The paper has also been named the state's best weekly in its circulation class in the annual newspaper show.

Zender and his wife Sue live in Carey. They have three daughters.